INSURANCE : A GENERAL TEXTBOOK

INSURANCE : A GENERAL TEXTBOOK

ABHISHEK GUPTA

CYBER TECH PUBLICATIONS
4264/3, Ansari Road, Daryaganj, New Delhi-110002 (India)
Ph.: 011-23244078, 011-43559448 Fax: 011-23280028
E-Mail: cyberpublicationsdelhi@yahoo.com
Website: www.cybertechpublications.com

INSURANCE : A GENERAL TEXTBOOK

ABHISHEK GUPTA

First Edition 2011

Published by :

G.S. Rawat for **Cyber Tech Publications**
4264/3, Ansari Road, Daryaganj, New Delhi-110002 (India)
Ph.: 011-23244078, 011-43559448 Fax: 011-23280028
E-Mail: cyberpublicationsdelhi@yahoo.com
Website: www.cybertechpublications.com

CONTENTS

Preface

1. An Overview 1
2. Real Facts of Life Insurance 24
3. Furure Prospects of Insurance 55
4. Theory of Insurance 93
5. Present Status of Insurance 122
6. Annual Reports of LIC and GIC 135
7. Insurance Concepts in General Life 228

Bibliography 260

Index 261

PREFACE

Life Insurance in India was nationalised by incorporating Life Insurance Corporation (LIC) in 1956. All private life insurance companies at that time were taken over by LIC. In 1993 the Government of Republic of India appointed RN Malhotra Committee to lay down a road map for privatisation of the life insurance sector. While the committee submitted its report in 1994, it took another six years before the enabling legislation was passed in the year 2000, legislation amending the *Insurance Act* of 1938 and legislating the *Insurance Regulatory and Development Authority Act* of 2000.

The same year that the newly appointed insurance regulator-Insurance Regulatory and Development Authority IRDA—started issuing licenses to private life insurers. Privatization of insurance sector has allowed insurance companies to work in the market by depositing 100 crore rupees in the reserve of government. This has encouraged many overseas insurance companies, having a required amount in their reserve, to open their branch in our country. Introduction of the sector has changed the employment pattern, but people must know how to make profit from it. To be in the global market and have advantage of it, capital and skill as per the demand and knowledge of market is the requirement. It is necessary that institutions, which form a part of this financial system, have internal management, governance and accountability structures, which measure up to the highest standards.

—Author

1

AN OVERVIEW

Insurance is the study of risk financing through risk pooling. In a dynamic economy like the one we have in Hong Kong, a myriad of things can go wrong everyday with our life, our health, our home, our car, and our business. The use of insurance to reduce the adverse financial impact in case of a loss has become an important element of financial planning in our society.

Risk management, as a building block of financial planning, seeks to identify the risks a person or a business faces and evaluating their financial impacts in case of occurrence. Once the relevant risks have been identified, the risk manager must determine the need for insurance based on his financial goal and assess the various risk handling tools available to him in order to select the one that can best serve his financial goal.

In order to make a sound risk management decision, the risk manager must have a thorough understanding of the designs and functions of various insurance products available for loss reduction and the new products and future trends of development in insurance.

This course deals with the analysis of financial and business exposures to loss and risk management techniques, the risk meeting alternatives and their economic, legal, and social implications, and the role of insurance in risk management. The proper functioning of insurance relies heavily on the validity of the legal contract between the insured and the insurer. This course will also explain the characteristics of the contractual agreements pertaining to each type of insurance product. Moreover, it will explain to students the major theories underlying each type of product that are essential for the risk manager to effectively conduct the cost and benefit analysis on the risk managment program.

For example, how are premiums for life insurance policies determined and how do we compare the costs of different policies that are compatible with our need? In addition to the analysis of insurance from the consumer's perspective, this course will also explain to students the structure of the insurance industry and its impact on the pricing of insurance products.

INSURANCE IN PRACTICE-BUSINESS RISKS

Some markets for business risks seem to work well. Businesses own property, for example, and most businesses insure at least some portions of that property. There is not very good data on the extent of this insurance, but studies of the industry suggest that this insurance is generally believed to work well. This is not surprising, since large businesses have individuals who specialize in the purchase of insurance, and even small businesses usually have some financial expertise. Predominantly on a secondary reference basis, we rate this insurance as good on our scale.

Businesses also have general liabilities associated with damages they may incur in the cost of doing business (people falling in the store, for example, or doctors being sued over health harms they cause). The performance of this insurance varies by industry. If we take account of both drama and policy import, the situation is particularly problematic in medical malpractice.

There have been three medical malpractice crises in the past 25 years: one in the mid-1970s, another in the mid-

1980s, and a third in just the past two years (Mello and Studdert, 2003). Each crisis was precipitated by claims paid increasing more rapidly than premium increases. The cause was changes in the social climate, not in any upswing in adverse medical incidents. Lawsuits filed increased more rapidly than expected, and liability judgments awarded were greater than expected.

As a result, insurers lost money. In response, premiums rose precipitously, many insurers dropped out of the market, many physicians found insurance difficult to obtain, and some physicians changed their practices (e.g., some OBGYNs quit doing obstetrics). Only after a few years did the market return to reasonable function, with insurance again available-albeit at higher price. This type of availability crisis, though often with no return to normalcy, is a common theme of many types of business insurance.

Risks with residual variability: environment and terrorism. In theory, as we noted above, insurance is best equipped to deal with small to moderate probability, high loss risks, for there is where it does the most good. However, it is for precisely those risks where business insurance has failed most recently. Environmental liability was the classic issue here (General Accounting Office, 1986; 1988; Huber, 1988; Zagaski, 1992); terrorism losses have recently joined it. In each case, private markets turned out to work much less well than anticipated, once the risks eventuated. We discuss these two risks in turn.

Prior to the mid-1980s, environmental coverage insured firms indefinitely for events that occurred during the policy year (termed an occurrence-based policy). Long-term risk was thought to be small. Total claims in the 1962, for example, were less than $XXX. Events in the 1970s and 1980s, however, highlighted the "long-tailed" nature of risk. Asbestos claims in the 1970s, for example, dealt with exposure to asbestos in the 1940s and 1950s. Added to this was the perception that legal interpretations were seen as changing the provisions of insurance policies. It was frequently asserted that courts ignored restrictions in policies to "sudden and accidental" environmental damage. Moreover, the courts, usually on the basis of jury decisions, imposed liabilities well beyond those the policy was intended to cover.

The result was increased uncertainty about the liability of environmental insurers.

In theory, an increase in risk should increase demand for insurance, increase the price of insurance, and result in greater overall coverage at higher prices. This was not the outcome with environmental risk, however, as it was not with medical malpractice insurance. Rather, the policies themselves changed in a way that made them less generous. For example, the occurrence-based policy was dropped in favor of a claims-made policy, which covers damages only if the claim is filed within a certain period of time.

Effectively, this eliminates insurance coverage for long-tail risk, placing that risk instead on the insuring firm, in the form of increases in premiums as the extent of damages is realized. Indeed, the reduction in insurance coverage was not limited to primary insurance markets. In 1984, international reinsurance markets began denying coverage for pollution liability reinsurance.

Insurers also imposed aggregate dollar limits on payouts for environmental damage, to limit their overall risk exposure. Of course, this is denying protection precisely where it is needed most, for high losses.

These changes limited the aggregate risk born by the insurer, with the consequence that more of the risk was retained by the firms at risk. Even two decades after the liability revolution and the initial cutbacks in insurance coverage, the market for environment insurance is substantially less generous than it was.

The 'crisis' in terrorism insurance burst onto the scene on September 11, 2001. The attacks that day drastically changed expectations about the likelihood and magnitude of terrorism losses in the future. Unlike nature's extreme blows, e.g., Hurricane Andrew, which can increase perceived future losses by say 100%, the man-made loss of 9/11 increased future expected terror losses at least by a factor of 10, perhaps much more. The immediate result was a crisis in insurance availability. Insurers claimed that terrorism was 'uninsurable', and stopped writing coverage for it. About one-quarter of policies written in 2002, an even larger share for large firms, excluded terrorist acts.

Though the most dire predictions about the consequences of lost insurance did not come true--buildings got built and buildings traded hands-the potential for severe economic disruption was judged to be high. After several months, the Federal government stepped in to stabilize the market. The Terrorism Risk Insurance Act of November 2002 provides for coverage related to international terrorism, with the Federal contribution rising with the magnitude of loss up through $100 billion of insured losses. Beyond that, the Congress decides what additional payments it wants to make.

In exchange for taking the back-end risk (without coinsurance), the Act requires insurers to write coverage for smaller terrorist losses. The Act sunsets at the end of 2005, and it is not clear what will happen in the market beyond that point. Employment practice insurance. Many businesses also have insurance for employment liability resulting from claims such as sexual harassment and race or gender lawsuits. As the potential liability from employment issues has become more widespread, the cost of this insurance has increased. As Table 6 shows, a business with 20 full-time employees and 20 part-time employees, for example, would pay a premium of $5,000 per year and have a 10 percent coinsurance rate.

There is also a limit on insurer liability, generally at $1,000,000. We do not know of general assessments of this line of insurance, however, so we omit it from the table.

Pension obligations. One of the more important long-term risks that firms face is over their obligations to retirees. Many firms, particularly large manufacturers, have substantial defined benefit pension obligations. Firms also have obligations for retiree health insurance. These obligations are risky because retirement experience and the earnings on pension assets are both uncertain.

Insurance for these risks is affected by a substantial degree of moral hazard. Firms that are doing poorly have the option of declaring bankruptcy and defaulting on their pension liabilities, rather than continuing to pay them. As a result of this moral hazard, pension risk is insured by the government. The Pension Benefit Guarantee Corporation (PBGC) requires firms to contribute an annual premium based partly on the number of retirees and partly on the degree of pension underfunding.

Like many government programs, the PBGC has difficulty changing prices to guarantee solvency. This is particularly difficult since pension default is a long-tailed risk: premiums taken in today need to be saved for potentially high use in the future. Boyce and Ippolito (2002) estimate that premiums charged by the PBGC are 50 percent below what equivalent private insurance rates would be, with unfunded liabilities currently over $100 billion. For these reasons, the General Accounting office rated the PBGC as high-risk.

Because participation in the PBGC is mandatory, we lose the yardstick of what private insurance would charge for equivalent coverage. And because it is effectively subsidized, there is little complaint. For these reasons, we rate the operation of pension insurance as poor.

Summary. Businesses are much more sophisticated than individuals about the purchase of insurance, with professionals handling the task in large firms. For traditional risks, insurance works well. Recent years, however, have witnessed the rise of risks due to purposeful human activity, e.g., the liability revolution or terrorism. These risks are larger than older risks, are correlated across insuring firms, and are often not resolved for many years. For such risks, insurance markets tend to work poorly.

NON-STANDARD BEHAVIOR ON THE DEMAND SIDE

Theory and practice diverge in the insurance industry for a second reason: potential insureds engage in non-standard economic behavior. In traditional decision theory, people have concave utility functions defined over consumption. Risk averse people will want to insure against all risks, assuming fair actuarial pricing. They temper this because of moral hazard and administrative costs, which lead prices to exceed expected payouts. In response, people will choose to cover large risks, at least substantially, and leave small risks unprotected.

Such preferences may not correspond to reality, however, as the prevalence of insurance coverage for small risks suggests. Several alternatives to standard preferences have been proposed that may explain this type of coverage. Prospect theory. A leading possibility is loss aversion-the idea that people significantly dislike any loss, even small ones (Kahneman and Tversky, 1979). Hence, people will pay far above actuarial value to protect against small losses, such as those when a stereo breaks.

HEALTH

Health risk is the second major type of risk for individuals. We divide health risks into two categories: short-term risks, and long-term risks.

Short-term Health Risks

Most people have health insurance for current medical care needs. About 85 percent of people have some form of health insurance in the United States. Coverage rates are greater in most other major developed nations, usually because of government involvement.

As with mortality risk, there has been substantial analysis of the optimality of private health insurance contracts. The fact that not everyone has private insurance has generated policy debate and research attention. There are three typical explanations for lack of coverage. The first is administrative expense. In any market with administrative costs, we would expect coverage to be less than full. Administrative costs are only about 15 percent of health insurance, however, so most analysts discount this explanation. Indeed, the true rate of administrative expense in health insurance is likely smaller, perhaps net negative in many instances when buyer leverage is figured in. Health insurers-with their strong bargaining power in a high fixed-cost industry-purchase specific health care goods and services much more cheaply than do individuals. Such discounts likely more than make up for administrative costs.

Adverse selection provides a second explanation. Insurance priced for the average enrolled person can lead to an equilibrium where the healthy do not enroll. We know of no simulations about the importance of this phenomenon, but we suspect that this explanation is right for some people. Many of the uninsured are young and relatively healthy. The value of insurance priced at average rates would not be very high for this group. One concern about this explanation, though, is that insurance can vary along the intensive margin as well. Deductibles, services covered, and access to particular providers all vary across policies, and we might expect more of the healthy to segregate into less generous policies than go without coverage entirely. The third explanation is crowdout by government insurance programs (for example Medicaid) and charitable programs, e.g., hospital free care.

In this theory, people do not purchase private coverage because they know that they can receive care even if uninsured. Naturally, there is a loss. Being uninsured is associated with less, and less appealing, access to medical care providers, less use of preventive and acute care services, and worse health outcomes (Institute of Medicine, 2003). But it also saves money.

For some people, the savings may be worth it. Empirical evidence shows that crowd-out is a factor in explaining insurance coverage. Increases in the generosity of public insurance (Cutler and Gruber, 1996), and in uncompensated care (Rask and Rask, 2000; Herring, 2001) lead more people to go uninsured. The type of analysis necessary to explain how much of the total number of uninsured this accounts for has not been undertaken, however.

Even were the level of health insurance appropriate, one might question the mix of provision between public and private. Insurance has a surprising mixture of such provision, in a pattern hardly in line with notions of comparative advantage across sectors. In the case of health insurance, some argue for public insurance, on the grounds that administrative costs are lower in public programs than in private policies (Woolhandler and Himmelstein, 1989).

Others argue for private insurance, for the usual reasons of competition and concern over bureaucracy. And within the private sector, there are arguments for both for-profit and not-for-profit entities. The US has a mixture of both public and private, often in the same narrow sector, with adverse interactions between the two (as witnessed by the crowd-out literature).

Among people who have insurance, economists' greatest concern has not been over inadequate coverage, but rather over the generosity of coverage people have for small medical risks. Cost sharing in traditional indemnity insurance policies is relatively low. A typical policy has a deductible of about $300, with 20 percent coinsurance up to a stop-loss of perhaps $1,500 (Kaiser Family Foundation and Health Research and Education Trust, 2003). For much of the health spending distribution, cost sharing will be very slight; this makes moral hazard a significant concern.

A lengthy literature has explored whether this structure of cost sharing is optimal or too small (see Cutler and Zeckhauser, 2000, for a review). Generally, the literature concludes that current insurance is too generous, leaving people with too little risk for medical expenses, particularly smaller expenses. The most comprehensive analysis is from Blomqvist (1997), who finds that optimal insurance should have a declining coinsurance rate ranging from 27 percent at $1,000 of spending (compared to 20 percent in most plans) down to 5 percent at $30,000 of spending (compared to zero in most plans). The traditional explanation for the low rate of cost sharing is the tax subsidy to health insurance (Feldstein and Friedman, 1977; Pauly, 1986). As with life insurance, employer payments for health insurance are not taxed as income to workers, while wage and salary payments are. Thus, there are incentives for people to run more medical payments through employer-paid health insurance than is optimal. This includes having lower cost-sharing than would otherwise be desirable. Empirical work shows that this explanation is important in practice (Cutler and Zeckhauser, 2000). What other factors contribute to low cost sharing is not known, however.

Behavioral explanations, which we explore at length subsequently, also merit study for low cost sharing. Fuchs (19xx), for example, argues that cost sharing is low in part because people do not want to make decisions about whether additional medical care is worth the money. We argue below that prospect-theoretic preferences for outcomes, e.g., loss aversion and risk seeking on losses, make individuals eager to avoid small losses.

We note that these types of behavioral explanations make normative analysis difficult. Say that loss aversion affected behavior, implying that even small per-visit charges strongly discourage use. Would such copayments represent an effective rationing tool, or would it be imposing noticeable pain without collecting much revenue? Fortunately, our analysis has a descriptive, not normative, purpose.

Finally, given HMOs strong penetration of the private insurance market and their firm supply-side restrictions, we note that it is hard to assess what appropriate cost sharing should be for their members.

Long-term Health-care Insurance

Health also has a long-term risk component. People may have health needs in the future, which they would like to insure today. Most important here is long-term care expenses; the magnitude of these expenses was noted earlier.

A large part of the return to long-term care insurance is related to early mortality among the elderly. Nearly 20 percent of people over age 85 are in a nursing home, compared to about 1 percent of the population aged 65 to 74. For long-term care insurance to be effective, people have to purchase before they reach advanced ages. Yet, most elderly do not have such coverage. Only about 10 percent of the elderly possess long-term care insurance. The bulk of long-term care expenses are paid for out-of-pocket or by Medicaid.

Risk about future health type is related to long-term care risk. Health insurance for individuals or the groups they buy as part of is usually experience rated. Should health decline, a person's (or their company's) premium increases. Thus, one might expect people to purchase insurance against the risk of becoming high cost in the future (Pauly, Kunreuther, and Hirth, 1995; Cochrane, 1995; Cutler, 1996). In practice, however, we see virtually no insurance against the risk of becoming sick and facing higher annual premiums in the future.

Adverse selection and moral hazard no doubt contribute to the failure of this market, but we believe the theoretical elegance of these subjects has led economists to give them too much weight. Risk aversion certainly differs across people, and that is not so correlated with health status (many of the worried well want to purchase insurance, in addition to the currently sick). Ex ante moral hazard is also somewhat deterred because health declines, even if treated, lead to much worse states, for which compensating payments are not forthcoming.

Attention has instead focused on two alternatives. The first is crowd-out of private long-term care insurance by the public sector. The Medicaid program covers long-term care expenses for people with no private insurance who have exhausted their income and assets paying for long-term care services. People may thus rely on Medicaid, if it comes to that, or give away assets to qualify for Medicaid, rather than purchase private insurance (Pauly, 1990). Recent simulation work suggests that this explanation can explain a significant fraction of the lack of purchase of private nursing home insurance (Brown and Finkelstein, 2003). As with short-term health insurance, there seems to be an inefficient interaction between public and private insurance.

The second explanation for low insurance coverage is that these risks are non-diversifiable, and thus shunned by insurance companies (Cutler, 1996). The dominant driver of changes in long-term care costs over time is technology that allows people to live longer or higher quality lives, but at high cost. This technology is common across people, and thus cannot be diversified cross-sectionally. We explore how this might affect the supply of long-term insurance below.

Summary. We rate coverage of short-term health risks as fair and coverage of long-term risks as poor. Short-term risks are covered for most people, but as with mortality risk there is both underprotection (those without coverage) and overprotection (too generous insurance in indemnity policies). Coverage for long-term health risks is poor, since private insurance is rare and the public sector has substantial inefficiencies.

Property

The third major type of individual risk is for property damage for personal physical assets. People insure their home, car, and consumer durables against various types of damages. In at least the first two cases, essentially everyone has coverage. Homeowners insurance is generally required by mortgage lenders, and all states require auto insurance. Fewer people have coverage for consumer durables, but the costs of these durables are far smaller, hence insurance is far less valuable.

The major issue in property insurance is the degree of cost sharing. Most people have relatively low deductibles for home and auto damage. The question is whether these deductibles are too low, from the standpoint of the individual and the standpoint of efficiency. (Efficiency requires avoiding little claims where administrative costs are large relative to any loss or payment.) There is speculation about this in the literature, but no formal analysis that we are aware of.

As with any evaluation dependent on the parameters of the utility function, we cannot say for certain whether consumers should or should not purchase more generous coverage. But we can evaluate what set of preferences are required to justify current purchases. Suppose that the probability of a loss is p. The loss may be damage to a car or house. For the simple algebra here, we assume the loss probability is independent of the details of the insurance policy.

EXPLANATIONS FOR POOR PERFORMANCE

Insurance in practice differs substantially from insurance in theory. Despite rating many insurance markets as likely to work well in theory, only one of the actual markets we evaluate draws a 'good' rating-homeowners insurance. Four markets get a fair rating (life insurance, short-term health insurance, auto insurance, and general business property and casualty insurance). The remaining six risks (annuities, long-term health risks, consumer durable insurance, and business environmental, terrorism and pension coverage) all rate poorly. While some may quibble with our ratings in particular cases, we suspect that none would disagree with our overall assessment of substantial underperformance in actual insurance markets.

The discrepancy between theory and practice is of two types. The first is a mismatch between expected coverage and actual coverage. Some risks that we expect to be covered, such as terrorism risk, long-term health risk, longevity risk, or environmental liability risk, are covered not at all, or at best poorly. Even risks that are covered well, such as life insurance, are not purchased by everyone who seems like they could benefit from them.

In contrast, many risks that theory would predict to be uncovered, such as small losses for automobiles, houses, and consumer durables, are covered by individuals voluntarily purchasing insurance. Assuming rational decision, only excessively high degrees of risk aversion could explain the pattern of property coverage that we observe. Further, many elderly seem overinsured against unexpected death (life insurance) even as they are underinsured against beyond-average survival (annuitization).

In addition, there is little rhyme or reason to the mix between public and private coverage. To be sure, many of the largest risks, such as terrorism, have made their way into the public sector, as one might expect. But smaller risks are covered publicly as well (flood insurance, for example), and many large risks are left to private insurers (environmental damage).

A common but troubling phenomenon is severe underpricing of risk coverage by the public sector, often because premiums are insufficiently responsive to risk differentials. Savings and loan insurance prior to the multi hundred billion dollar bailout is a good example. When politics and political pressures intrude, it is often impossible to impose significant differential rates for insurance. Often government just sets a risk standard to be met if one wants to insure. Such standards are often ambiguous, and government denial of insurance is often too much of a nuclear weapon.

The interactions between public and private insurance seem unhelpful at best, harmful at worst.

There a number of complementary explanations for the mismatch between insurance theory and insurance markets in practice. We explore them in the next sections.

Information-Based Explanations

The explanation favored by most economists (casual polls suggest) is asymmetric information. Insurers may not offer particular products because they worry that it will affect the behavior of insureds (moral hazard), or because they fear that the product will be selected by people who have a high likelihood of suffering a loss (adverse selection). Such "bad behavior" cannot be monitored.

These explanations contribute, but we suspect that they are far from sufficient. For many of the risks that are uncovered, such as long-term environmental exposure by firms or the need for long-term care, evidence of moral hazard is at best tenuous. Where we are certain there is moral hazard is for use at a point in time, short-term health care for instance. This risk is covered, if anything, too well.

Nor is adverse selection much of an explanation. Evidence to date suggests no adverse selection in long-term care insurance purchases, for example (Finkelstein and McGarry, 2003). While adverse selection has dominated the theoretical literature, the actual experience of an insurer-what we think of as 'adverse experience'-depends on many factors beyond perceived risk. Risk aversion is important: the worried well purchase insurance just as much as the high risk. As a side benefit, this keeps premiums low for those on the margin of purchase.

Indeed, risk aversion may be inversely correlated with risk levels, if risk averse people take better care to avoid putting themselves in risky situations. Ignorance is also a blessing here. If potential insureds do not know their risk levels, there will be no correlation between risk and the insurance decision.

More generally, non-rational behavior helps deter adverse selection. It introduces many new elements that encourage people to insure, without necessarily being correlated with risk. In many situations, we might expect that insurers would know more about risks than individuals. This is likely the case with consumer durable warranties, and possibly health insurance as well. Variation in price by risk status limit adverse selection, though they may be inefficient in other ways (denying people insurance over their risk level).

The limited explanatory power of asymmetric information-based explanations show up most clearly in the analysis of terrorism insurance.

By all assessments, there is little to no differential information about the likelihood of terrorists striking any particular object (adverse selection) nor is it plausible that firms would substantially lower their guard against terrorist attack (moral hazard) just because they are insured. (The uncompensable losses, including one's own loss of life, are just too great.) Insurance coverage dried up for other reasons.

Our more general hypothesis is that in many markets where we might speculate that adverse selection would exert a powerful undertow on the market, it proves to be more mild current than sweeping tide. We propose three alternative reasons why the theory and practice of insurance diverge in the early 21st century.

Incomplete Diversification, Supply-side Contracting Difficulties

The first explanation is insufficient diversification of insurance companies. People may want insurance against a risk, but insurers have to be willing to provide that risk, even at rates far above the best estimates of actuarial cost. If insurers-or more accurately insurance executives--are worried about their capitalization, they may be unwilling to write policies for some risks, even if both price and demand are high. The prospect of severe losses, or even bankruptcy with its limited liability, may not scare the diversified investors in an insurance company, who would be happy to write unusual insurance for robust premiums. But insurance executives have to worry that they may be considered to have misestimated risks and premiums, with consequent career collapse. In the standard theory of insurance, risks are minimally correlated across insureds.

A few people will experience a loss in a period, but the vast majority will not. Insurers use the premiums from those who do not suffer a loss to compensate those who do. Many risks, however, have an aggregate component, many people incur a loss at the same time. Nuclear wars represented the ultimate aggregate risk for many years. Today's aggregate risks include new liability revolutions (as with environmental damage), significant increases in prices (say for medical care), and major terrorist attacks.

Even good developments have their aggregate risk component. Thus, rapid rises in longevity would impose heavy aggregate costs on pensions and other annuities. Long-term care insurance well represents an aggregate risk: When the expected costs increase for one person, say because a longevity jump makes nursing home stays, particularly Alzheimer stays, more expensive, this factor applies to many insureds. As a result, the traditional method of risk diversification, pooling independent risks across people, fails.

Risk neutral insurers will not care about this aggregate risk. The owners of insurance company assets can diversify the risk posed by diversifying their portfolio. But managers and workers in those insurance companies may care. Their jobs may be lost if the company goes bankrupt, or if that line of business loses gobs of money. Thus, the insurance company itself may behave as if risk averse.

A moderately risk-averse insurance company will still sell insurance, but will impose a higher administrative charge to do so. Administrative loads in long-term care insurance, which has a large contingent of aggregate risk, are 35 percent at minimum, and reach 50 to 70 percent for some groups (Cutler, 1996; Brown and Finkelstein, 2003). In comparison, administrative costs in short-term health insurance are only about 15 percent (United States General Accounting Office, 1984), roughly their level for annuities (Mitchell, Poterba, Warshawsky, and Brown, 1999).

An insurer that is more risk averse than potential insureds will refuse to write insurance altogether. We often see this in the nature of risk exposure that is written. When they do write policies, long-term care insurers limit their exposure to a fixed dollar amount per day of nursing home care; one cannot buy coverage for the actual cost of care received (in contrast to annual health insurance). Similarly, environmental insurers and medical malpractice insurers refuse to cover all claims that result from operations today; instead, they put a time limit on when the claim must be filed.

The cycle of insurance crises shows clearly this problem. When risks increase more than expected-e.g., the liability revolution, knowledge of particular chemical harms, terrorist action-insurers respond at first by refusing to write new risk. That is understandable, as markets digest the new information. Over time, prices rise. That too is predictable. But even after the market 'settles down', insurance frequently becomes less generous than it was formerly, and stays that way indefinitely. That is the part that is economically unpredicted.

While the practice may appear to be irrational economically, the idea of severely curtailing company risk is standard advice given in the insurance industry. According to A.M. Best (1991), a leading analyst of the insurance industry, insurers should keep the risk of any line of business small. "[T]o provide stability and safety, an insurer should limit its maximum loss exposure on a single risk (or group of related risks) to a small percentage of its policyholders' surplus, normally less than 2 percent" (p. xiii). With aggregate risks, insurers face the Scylla and Charybdis of not knowing their market, or having too heavy exposure. The outcome is that the insurance industry does not write certain classes of risk.

For some risks the government may step in, as it has with terrorism risk. But that is a short-term (three-year) solution, it is as an adjunct to other private-sector insurance, and it is in an area where the government could be deemed to have responsibility for controlling the risk. Government as reinsurer is not a likely solution for many troubling aggregate risks, such as long-term environment or health-care risks.

Fortunately, there is a far greater pool of resources that could conceivably absorb such risks. It is found in financial markets. Risks that are large even for the world's insurance pool-estimated to be on the order of $1 trillion in the United States and $2 trillion worldwide (Insurance Information Institute, 2003)-are small relative to financial markets. For example, the value of equity markets in the US alone is more than $10 trillion. One great advantage of financial markets as insurance instruments, apart from their volume, is that they effectively bring together tens of millions of investors, none of whom would have to hold too much of an aggregate risk.

There has been recent use of financial markets to diversify aggregate insurance risks. Most prominent have been catastrophe bonds, used to reinsure weather-related housing risks. Interest in these bonds rose with Hurricane Andrew in 1992, the Northridge earthquake in 1994, and the Kobe, Japan earthquake in 1995, all involving losses that were massive relative to historical experience.

The market for catastrophe bonds has been relatively small, but it is perceived to be successful (United States General Accounting Office, 2002). One measure of success is the prices charged. Famed investor Warren Buffett underwrote earthquake reinsurance in California for four years in the early 1990s, earning an 11 percent premium for an estimated 1 percent risk. Buffett recognized what other insurers must have missed: This risk, though unusual, brought neither adverse selection nor moral hazard. Over time, the advantage of this investment became known and premiums fell. "The influx of 'investor' money into catastrophe bonds-which may well live up to their name-has caused super-cat prices to deteriorate materially. Therefore, we will write less business in 1998", Buffett wrote. Use of these new instruments is not without problems. Participation of insurance companies is likely to be important, since these companies have expertise in assessing risk that is vital. Possibly, insurance companies will underwrite the risks initially, to provide their assessment expertise for a fee, and investors will then take their share. Reinsurance is already common in the insurance industry, though it is typically done by specialized companies rather than broader financial markets. Perhaps more importantly, the nature of the payment needs to be determined. Investment managers are currently paid for assuming risk. The common arrangement is for the general partner to charge an annual management fee, say 1 percent, and to receive 20 percent of the profits or excess profits. With insurance, equivalent arrangements would be hard to structure, since risks are discrete and it is hard to know whether a policy issued has been profitable in expectation thus far. If there is a 3 percent chance of a calamitous event, for example, but otherwise no losses, a general partner paid on the basis of annual "profits" would be expected to do quite well for a period before the odds brought down the house. Further compounding the difficulty, prior management and incentive fees would probably be unrecoverable in the event of a bad loss. Many of the names at Lloyds of London experienced just such a string-many small successes followed by a mammoth loss-when the liability revolution hit. One way around this problem would be to have the portfolio of risks be highly diversified. But such diversification blunts the value of specialized expertise on the market being insured. Other types of contracts may be needed. With additional time, we expect that financial instruments will continue to evolve and allow further investors into the market. It is possible-perhaps likely-that the first problem we identify has a solution forthcoming.

CONCLUSION

The fundamental principle of insurance demand is that coverage becomes more valuable as the variability of potential outcomes grows. In the 1960s, prescription drug costs were low, and there was little risk associated with buying medications. It made little sense to include prescription drugs in coverage. By 2003, the risks for the elderly were much greater. Even though the costs to the government of the new benefit were high, the potential risk-spreading value made it worthwhile. The United States government recently enacted the largest expansion in health insurance coverage in a generation. In November 2003, the Medicare program, set up in the 1960s and largely the same today as then, was enriched by the addition of an outpatient prescription drug benefit. In many ways, adding prescription drugs to Medicare represented a triumph of economic reasoning. Alas, effective risk sharing was not fully enshrined in the new legislation.

Indeed, the cost sharing in the new legislation is, by economic considerations, somewhat bizarre. Elderly enrolling in the new program face a $250 deductible. After that, the government pays 25 percent of the bill up to $2,250 in total spending. The government then ceases payment until total spending reaches $5,100 ($3,600 of individual costs). Above that amount, the government pays 95 percent and the individual 5 percent. There is no upper limit on individual spending.

From a risk-spreading perspective, a far more valuable insurance policy would have individuals cover more of the up-front costs, and leave the government to take more of the back-end liability. Politics no doubt helps to explain the benefits structure, probably derived from the type of utility anomalies discussed above. A certainty equivalent benefit of $110, where the actual monies go to 10 percent of the elderly population may be politically less effective than a certainty equivalent benefit of $100 where a large share of the money is spent among the vast part of the population. The new legislation also considers the issue of public and private insurance, but here too the answer seems strange. Why didn't the private sector ever offer insurance for prescription drugs if that coverage is so valuable? The answer is that drug benefits are almost a poster child for adverse selection. The elderly with high drug needs know who they are, and they would raise the cost of private drug coverage beyond what the vast majority of elderly would consider paying.

Given sufficient skewness in expenditure, the market unravels. Still, the new legislation envisions the majority of the elderly obtaining coverage through private insurance companies offering stand-alone pharmaceutical coverage. The classic economic solution to adverse selection-single payer health insurance-was explicitly rejected as being too regulatory a solution. To partly offset the selection incentives induced, the legislation includes a substantial sum to give to employers already providing drug coverage-28 percent of costs between $250 and $5,000 per person. It is not known if this subsidy will prevent crowdout any more than previous subsidies to the poor through Medicaid.

We also identify possible solutions. Encouraging greater risk spreading beyond the narrow confines of primary insurance and reinsurance is a central one. Sometimes, government and private firms collaborate in this venture, as in terrorism insurance, where the government is a reinsurer. More generally, financial markets represent an enormous pool of largely-untapped potential insurance dollars. The future, we are confident, will confront significant new risks, and will develop new mechanisms for spreading them. Alas, neither the invisible hand nor sophisticated theories of insurance will assure that the right entities write the right coverage for the right insureds.

Our theories of insurance must be elaborated to capture realities on the ground, including the factors that motivate entities to insure. Insurance practice should be adjusted to meet realistic expectations of how risks can be spread effectively. This ongoing minuet of adjustments, perhaps a dance over decades, should allow the theory and practice of insurance to reunite Unfortunately (for economists), the seeming anomalies in the Medicare drug benefit are more common than we would care to admit. Exploring a number of insurance policies in practice, we argue that the conventional theory of insurance misses reality in two respects. First, it assumes near risk neutrality on the supply-side of the market, when in fact strong risk aversion is more appropriate, particularly given agency concerns of insurance decision makers. Second, we show that many attributes of insurance equilibrium can best be explained if people's behavior diverges from the rational model. They have non-standard preferences-e.g., they care about even tiny losses; they seek to equate utility across states not marginal utility; they disproportionately buy coverage for risks that are "available"..

2

REAL FACTS OF LIFE INSURANCE

IMPORTANCE OF LIFE INSURANCE

Life Insurance is of great importance to individuals, groups, business community and general public. As Discussed before, Insurance is a contract in writing under which insurer agrees in return for a consideration (premium) to indemnify the insured against the loss suffered on account of an uncertain future event. Life insurance is a contract for payment of a sum of money to the person assured on the occurrence of the event insured by the contract. Some of the main benefits of life insurance are given below.

Protection against untimely Death

Life insurance provides protection to the dependents of the life insured and the family of the assured in case of his untimely death. The dependents or family members get a fixed sum of money in case of death of the assured.

Saving for Old Age

After retirement the earning capacity of a person reduces. Life insurance enables a person to enjoy peace of mind and a sense of security in his/her old age.

Promotion of Savings

Life insurance encourages people to save money compulsorily. When a life policy is taken, the assured is to pay premiums regularly to keep the policy in force and he cannot get back the premiums, only surrender value can be returned to him. In case of surrender of policy, the policyholder gets the surrendered value only after the expiry of duration of the policy.

Initiates Investments

Life Insurance Corporation encourages and mobilizes the public savings and channelises the same in various investments for the economic development of the country. Life insurance is an important tool for the mobilization and investment of small savings.

Credit Worthiness

Life insurance policy can be used as a security to raise loans. It improves the credit worthiness of business.

Social Security

Life insurance is important for the society as a whole also. Life insurance enables a person to provide for education and marriage of children and for construction of house. It helps a person to make financial base for future.

Tax Benefit

Under the Income Tax Act, premium paid is allowed as a deduction from the total income under section 80C.

OBJECTIVES

After going through this unit you should be able to:

- Develop an understanding of life insurance basics and its importance
- Understand various types of life insurance policies offered by insurance companies
- Mention the suitability of various life insurance policies to different persons with variety of needs.

- Know various documents prepared by insurance company for a life insurance contract.
- Explain the procedure to handle death claims and maturity claims.
- Understand pricing objectives and elements of life insurance.
- Understand procedure of underwriting of new business

CONCEPT, DOCUMENTATION & CLAIM SETTLEMENT

Meaning and Importance Concept of Life Insurance: Life insurance is a contract under which the insurer (Insurance Company) in consideration of a premium paid undertakes to pay a fixed sum of money on the death of the insured or on the expiry of a specified period of time whichever is earlier. In case of life insurance, the payment for life insurance policy is certain.

The event insured against is sure to happen only the time of its happening is not known. So life insurance is known as 'Life Assurance'.

The subject matter of insurance is life of human being. Life insurance provides risk coverage to the life of a person. On death of the person insurance offers protection against loss of income and compensate the titleholders of the policy.

BASIC PRINCIPLES OF LIFE INSURANCE CONTRACT

Insurable Interest

The insured must have insurable interest in the life assured. In absence of insurable interest, Contract of insurance is void. Insurable interest must be present at the time of entering into contract with insurance company for life insurance. It is not necessary that the assured should have insurable interest at the time of maturity also.

Insurable interest exists in the following cases:

(a) A person has an unlimited insurable interest in his/her own life.

(b) A person has an insurable interest in the life of his/her spouse.

(c) A father has an insurable interest in the life of his son or daughter on whom he is dependent. Likewise a son may have insurable interest in life of his parents.

(d) A creditor has an insurable interest in the life of the debtor, to the extent of the debt.

(e) A servant employed for a specified period has insurable interest in the life of his employer.

Utmost good Faith

The contract of life insurance is a contract of utmost good faith. The insured should be open and truthful and should not conceal any material fact in giving information to the insurance company, while entering into a contract with insurance company. Misrepresentation or concealment of any fact will entitle the insurer to repudiate the contract if he wishes to do so.

Not a Contract of Indemnity

The life insurance contract is not a contract of indemnity. A Contract of life insurance is not a contract of indemnity. The loss of life cannot be compensated and only a fixed sum of money is paid in the event of death of the insured. So, the life insurance contract is not a contract of indemnity. The loss resulting from the death of life assured cannot be calculated in terms of money.

TYPES OF LIFE INSURANCE POLICIES

Life insurance policies can be grouped into the following categories:

Term Policy

In case of Term assurance plans, insurance company promises the insured for a nominal premium to pay the face value mentioned in the policy in case he is no longer alive during the term of the policy. Term assurance policy has the following features:

- It provides a risk cover only for a prescribed period. Usually these policies are short-term plans and the term ranges from one year onwards. If the policyholder survives till the end of this period, the risk cover lapses and no insurance benefit payment is made to him.
- The amount of premium to be paid for these policies is lower than all other life insurance policies. As savings and reserves are not accumulated under this policy, it has no surrender value and loan or paid-up values are not allowed on these policies.
- This plan is most suitable for those who are initially unable to pay high premium
- when income is low as required for Whole Life or Endowment policies, but requires life cover for a high amount.

WHOLE LIFE POLICY

This policy runs for the whole life of the assured. The sum assured becomes payable to the legal heir only after the death of the assured. The whole life policy can be of three types.

(1) Ordinary whole life policy – In this case premium is payable periodically throughout the life of the assured.

(2) Limited payment whole life policy – In this case premium is payable for a specified period (Say 20 Years or 25 Years) Only.

(3) Single Premium whole life policy – In this type of policy the entire premium is payable in one single payment.

ENDOWMENT LIFE POLICY

In this policy the insurer agrees to pay the assured or his nominees a specified sum of money on his death or on the maturity of the policy which ever is earlier. The premium for endowment policy is comparatively higher than that of the whole life policy. The premium is payable till the maturity of the policy or until the death of the assured which ever is earlier. It provides protection to the family against the untimely death of the assured.

HEALTH INSURANCE SCHEMES

An individual is subject to uncertainty regarding his health. He may suffer from ailments, diseases, disability caused by stroke or accident, etc. For serious cases the person may have to be hospitalized and intensive medical care has to be provided which can be very expensive. It is here that medical insurance is helpful in reducing the financial burden.

These days the vulnerability to lifestyle diseases such as heart, cancer, neurotic, and pollution based, etc are on the increase. So it makes sense for an individual to go for medical insurance cover.

JOINT LIFE POLICY

This policy is taken on the lives of two or more persons simultaneously. Under this policy the sum assured becomes payable on the death of any one of those who have taken the joint life policy. The sum assured will be paid to the survivor(s). For example, a joint life policy may be taken on the lives of husband and wife, sum assured will be payable to the survivor on the death of the spouse.

WITH PROFIT AND WITHOUT PROFIT POLICY

Under with profit policy the assured is paid, in addition to the sum assured, a share in the profits of the insurer in the form of bonus.

Without profit policy is a policy under which the assured does not get any share in the profits earned by the insurer and gets only the sum assured on the maturity of the policy. With profit and without profit policies are also known as participating and non –participating policies respectively.

DOUBLE ACCIDENT BENEFIT POLICY

This policy provides that if the insured person dies of any accident, his beneficiaries will get double the amount of the sum assured.

ANNUITY POLICY

Under this policy, the sum assured is payable not in one lump sum payment but in monthly, quarterly and half-yearly or yearly installments after the assured attains a certain age. This policy is useful to those who want to have a regular income after the expiry of a certain period e.g. after retirement. Annuity is paid so long as the assured survives. In annuity policy medical checkup is not required. Annuity is paid so long as the assured survives.

POLICIES FOR WOMEN

Women, now a days are free to take life assurance policies. However, some specially designed policies suit their needs in a unique manner; the synopsis of some these policies are as follows:

a. Jeevan Sathi is also known a Life Partner plan where the husband and wife are covered under this endowment policy, which gives the following benefits.

i. On maturity, provided both are alive, full sum assured with bonus is paid.

ii. On the death of one of the assured during the period of the policy, basic sum assured is paid to the surviving partner, who is not required to pay any further premiums.

iii. The surviving partner remains covered for the full sum assured. If she/he dies, then the sum assured is paid to the nominee, but this is before the maturity date.

iv. The surviving partner will be paid sum assured with bonuses if he survives till the maturity date. Hence this policy gives a comprehensive family protection.

b. Jeevan Sukanya is highlighted by the following points.

i. Only female child aged between 1 to 12 years is covered in this plan.

ii. band is automatically covered under the policy after marriage.

iii. Risk of the child starts either after 2 years of taking the policy or not before the age of 7, whichever is early.

iv. Premium paying period is 20 years minus age at entry.

v. On surviving the age of 20, the life assured receives the sum assured as survival benefit and the policy continues to cover the life assured till maturity date when vested bonus will be paid only. If life assured dies before maturity, sum assured with bonuses will be paid.

GROUP INSURANCE

Group life insurance is a plan of insurance under which the lives of many persons are covered under one life insurance policy. However, the insurance on each life is independent of that on the other lives. Usually, in group insurance, the employer secures a group policy for the benefit of his employees. Insurer provides coverage for many people under single contract.

POLICIES FOR CHILDREN

Policies for children are meant for the various needs of the children such as education, marriage, security of life etc. Some of the major children policies are:

(1) Children's deferred assurances

(2) Marriage endowment and educational annuity plans

(3) Children endowment policy

MONEY BACK POLICY

In this case policy money is paid to the insured in a number of separate cash payments. Insurer gives periodic payments of survival benefit at fixed intervals during the term of policy as long as the policyholder is alive.

Documentation

The contract for the life insurance starts with the proposal made by the proposer in standard application form available with insurance company and then various other documents are prepared.

PROPOSAL FORMS

The proposal form is a standardized form. The proposal form is a type of an application form, which a proposer has to fill all the relevant details about the life to be assured. The agent has the proposal form with him provided by the insurer. There are different types of policies and so the different types of proposal forms are there. It has the entire details regarding the duration of the policy, type of plan, mode of payment, etc. A proposal form is to be to be completed by the proposer in his own handwriting and signed in the presence of the agent. The proposal form contains a declaration at the end, to ensure the authenticity of the information given.

Usually the proposal form contains the following information to be filled by the prospective insured:

1. Name of life assured
2. Address
3. Date of Birth
4. Occupation
5. Age
6. Name of the employer (if any)
7. Sum assured of the proposed policy
8. Number and age of the family members
9. Family medical history
10. Proposer's Medical history

Besides these there are other related forms regarding health, occupation, the agent's confidential report and many others. In addition there is a consent letter which shows the consent of the life assured to the imposition of some clause or extra premium, duly signed by the life assured.

FIRST PREMIUM RECEIPT

The agent provides the proposal form and other related documents and the underwriter examines the form and other documents and then determines the terms on which to accept the risk or reject the same.

The consent of the person assured is obtained in the form of payment of premium. After receiving the payment, the insurance company issues the First Premium Receipt, which acknowledges the proposal of the life-assured. It contains all particulars of the policy. It has the details of the next premium to be paid.

The policy bond is sent within 45-50 days from the date of first premium receipt to the life assured. The First Premium Receipt is an important and powerful document on the basis of which the life-assured can ask the insurer to issue the policy bond, which is treated as Evidence of the Contract of Life assurance.

POLICY BOND

After issuing the First Premium Receipt, the next step is that of the insurer of sending the policy bond to the life-assured and this document is also known as Policy Contract, which is the ultimate evidence of the life-assured.

The Policy Contract contains all the terms and conditions of the contract between insurance company and the life assured, duly stamped as per the Indian Stamp Act. The policy is sent to the life assured by the insurer. The policy contract contains the details of the insurance such as duration of the policy, the type of policy, sum assured, premium amount and the date of maturity, extra premium, nominee, assignee etc.

ALTERATIONS AND ENDORSEMENTS

Endorsement is an authenticated noting on the back of Policy Contract and forms a part of the contract. In the case of lack of space, the endorsements can be put on a separated sheet of papers and attached to the policy. Endorsements are required because life assurance is a long-term contract and the life assured may want certain changes in the terms of contract.

There are different type of alterations or modifications that can be made during the tenure of the policy such as changes regarding increase or reduction in the sum assured, mode of payment of premium, modification related on account of mistakes in the preparation of the policy by the insurer, modifications related to reduction in term, conversion from "Non-profit" to "With Profit" and similar other like change of name, plan-term and so on.

REMINDING NOTICE

It is basically information sent by the insurer to the policyholder, reminding the latter about the due date of a particular premium and the amount of premium. However it is not the duty of the insurance company (insurer) to do so. The insurer also informs the policyholder about the lapse of a policy if the premiums are not paid in time.

OTHER DOCUMENTS

Apart from other documents there are some other specialized documents, which are as follows:

i. Proposal on the lives of Non Resident Indians, which consists of some special questionnaire asking for relevant information.

ii. Partnership Insurance which consist of papers asking for the Profit & Loss account of the firm for the last three years, the insurance of the partner, the partnership deed and the deed of variation allowing the purchase of the assurance policy.

Settlement of Claims

The easy and timely settlement of a valid claim is an important function of an insurance company. The yardstick to judge insurance company's efficiency is as to how quick the claim settlement is. The speed, kindness and fairness with which an insurer handles claims show the maturity of the company and may lead to great satisfaction of the client. In every insurance company claim handling is of immense importance. It is the liability of the insurance company to honour valid and legal claims. At the same the company must identify the fraudulent and invalid claims. A claim may arise:

i) On death of Policyholder before the maturity date.

ii) On maturity, i.e. after expiry of the endowment period specified in the policy contract when the policy money becomes payable.

Certain features are common to all life insurance claims. These are:

1. Policy must be in force at the time of claims.
2. Insured must be covered by the policy.
3. Nothing was outstanding to the insurer at the time of claim.
4. Claim is covered by the policy.

DEATH CLAIMS

Intimation of Death

The death of the life assured has to be intimated in writing to the insurer. It can be done by the Assignee or nominee under the policy or from a person representing such Assignee or Nominee or when there is no nomination or assignment by a relative of the life assured, the employer, the agent or the development officer. Where policy is assigned to a creditor or a bank for valuable consideration, intimation of death may be received from such assignee. Sometimes, the office need not wait till the intimation of claim is received. The concerned agent, newspaper reports in case of accidents or air crashes, obituary columns may give information and claim action can be started. However, the identity of the deceased should be established carefully. The intimation of the death of the life assured by the claimant should contain the following particulars:

(1) his or her relationship with the deceased,

(2) the name of the policyholder,

(3) the number/s of the policy/policies,

(4) the date of death

(5) the cause of death and

(6) sum assured etc.

If any of these particulars are missing the claimant can be asked to furnish the same to the insurer. The intimation must satisfy two conditions (1) It must establish properly the identity of the deceased person as the life assured under the policy, (2) It must be from a concerned person.

Proof of Death and Other Documents

In case of claim by death, after the receiving the intimation of death the insurance company ensures that the insurance policy has been in force for the sum assured on the date of death and the intimation has been received from assignee, nominee or other claimant.

The following documents are required:

(i) Certificate of death.

(ii) Proof of age of the life assured (if not already given).

(iii) Deeds of assignment / reassignments.

(iv) Policy document.

(v) Form of discharge.

If the claim has accrued within three years from the beginning of the policy, the following additional requirements may be called for:

(i) Statement from the hospital if the deceased had been admitted to hospital.

(ii) Certificate of medical attendant of the deceased giving details of his/her last illness.

(iii) Certificate of cremation or burial to be given by a person of known character and responsibility present at the cremation or burial of the body of the deceased.

(iv) Certificate by employer if the deceased was an employee.

Proof of death and other documents to be submitted will depend upon the cause of death and circumstances of each case.

(1) In case of an air crash the certificate from the airline authorities would be necessary certifying that the assured was a passenger on the plane. In case of ship accident a certified extract from the logbook of the ship is required. In case of sudden cardiac arrest, murder the doctors' certificate may not be available.

(2) The insurance may waive strict evidence of title if the sum assured of the policy is small and there is no dispute among the survivors of the policy moneys.

(3) If the life assured had a death due to accident, suicide or unknown cause the police inquest report, panchanama, post mortem report, etc would be required.

If by any chance policy contract is lost, advertisement of the lost of policy is to be given. Payment can be made on the basis of an indemnity given by the policyholder. If the deceased has taken out policies with more than one branch and the claimant has produced proof of death to any one of them and desires that the other branch or branches, may act on the same proof, his request should be complied with. The Branch requiring proof of death should directly call for the certified copies from the branch concerned.

Net Payable Amount of Claim

After receiving the required documents the company calculates the amount payable under the policy. For this purpose, a form is filled in which the particulars of the policy, assignment, nomination, bonus etc. should be entered by reference to the Policy Ledger Sheet.

If a loan exists under the policy, then the section dealing with loan is contacted to give the details of outstanding loan and interest amount, which is deducted from the gross policy amount to calculate net payable claim amount. The net amount of claim payable is calculated and is called payment voucher. In the case of 'in force' policy unpaid premiums if any due before the Assured's death with late fee where necessary and the premium falling due in the policy year current at the time of death should be deducted from the claim amount.

MATURITY CLAIMS

If the life insured survives to the full term, then basic sum assured is payable. This payment by the insurer to the insured on the date of maturity is called maturity payment. The amount payable at the time of the maturity includes a sum assured and bonus/incentives. The insurer sends in advance the intimation to the insured with a blank discharge form for filling various details in it. It is to be returned to the office along with

- Original Policy document
- Age proof if age is not already submitted
- Assignment /reassignment, if any..

Legally no claim is acceptable in respect for a lapsed policy or death of the Life assured happening within 3 years from the date of beginning of the policy. However, some concessions are given and payment of claims is made:

- If the Life assured had paid at least 3 years' premiums and thereafter if premiums have not been paid, the nominees/life assured get proportionate paid up value.

- In the event of the death of' the Life assured within 3 years and the policy is under the lapsed position, nothing is payable.

PROCEDURE OF THE MATURITY CLAIMS

Settlement procedure for maturity claim is simple after receipt of completed and stamped discharge form from the person entitled to the policy money along with policy documents, claim amount will be paid by account payee cheque.

- If the life assured is reported to have died after the date of maturity but before the receipt is discharged, the claim is to be treated as the maturity claim and paid to the legal heirs. In this case death certificate and evidence of title is required.
- Where the assured is known to be mentally deranged, a certificate from the court of law under the Indian Lunacy Act appointing a person to act as guardian to manage the properties of the lunatic should be called.

ADDITIONAL BENEFITS APART FROM REGULAR CLAIMS

Double Accident Benefit: For claiming the benefits under the Double Accident Benefit the claimant has to produce the proof to the satisfaction of the Corporation that the accident is defined as per the policy conditions. Normally for claiming this benefit documents like FIR, Post-mortem Report are required.

Disability Benefit Claims include waiver of all premiums to be paid in future till the expiry of the policy of the life assured if a person is totally and permanently disabled and cannot earn any wage/compensation/profit as a result of the accident. Presently, all over the country there are 12 centers where the Insurance Ombudsman has been appointed. They are part of grievance redressal machinery. They consider the complaints regarding disputes related to premiums, claims etc.

UNDER WRITING AND SERVICING

Underwriting of New Business

One of the most important functions of the New Business Department is to decide whether to accept, postpone or decline a risk and to determine the terms to be offered if the risk is to be accepted. This is called underwriting or selection of risk. The underwriter has to evaluate the hazards associated with the risk, which is being proposed.

The life insurance underwriting is concerned with mortality rate and risk, i.e., the risk that the life insured may die before the maturity of the policy. Mortality risk depends upon the life insured's health, family medical history, nature of work etc. Underwriting is the insurance function that is responsible for assessing and classifying the degree of risk a proposer has and then deciding whether to accept or reject the risk.

UNDERWRITING PROCESS

The person willing to purchase the life insurance policy fills the proposal form. The proposal form along with the medical examiner's report and the other reports is checked and the risk associated with the case is calculated. After evaluation of risk, the insurer has following choices:

The insurance company may accept the proposal.

If a company decides to accept then the calculation regarding the premium to be charged from the proposer is to be made and terms and conditions are decided upon. The premium should be paid within a particular period specified by the insurer failing which the proposal stands cancelled.

The insurance company may reject the proposal

If the company decides not to accept the proposal then the proposer is informed accordingly. If the insurer decides to accept the proposal on special terms the proposer is informed accordingly.

The process of underwriting consists of following steps:

EVALUATION OF DOCUMENTS

1. The proposal papers will be complete when the proposal forms; medical examiner's report, agent's confidential report and personal statement are attached. In some cases medical examination may not be required. The question sin the proposal form must be answered with full honesty and no material fact should be concealed. The following particulars are generally required by the insurer:

   i) Age, Sex, Height and weight.

   ii) Occupation: The detailed information can be asked about the occupation if considered hazardous like aviation, electrical and chemical industry.

   iii) Other Policies: The number and amount of other policies of the proposer.

   iv) Premium to be paid and income of the proposer should be consistent, i.e., ensuring that proposer will not have any problem paying the premium of the policy.

   v) Date of Birth: The proposer who is either less than 20 years of age or more than 50 years of age should give satisfactory proof of age.

   vi) Risky habits of the proposer (Car racing etc)

   vii) Alcohol intake (Excessive intake of alcohol may affect the death probability of the proposer)

   viii) Frequency of foreign travel

ix) Marital status and number of children of proposer

x) Medical examiner's report

CLASSIFICATION AND REVIEW OF RISK

Once all of the information is available, underwriter from insurance company evaluates the data. At this evaluation, the underwriter wants to classify the risk attached to the proposal. If the risk is more than what the insurance company is willing to bear for that proposal, the application is rejected by the underwriter. If the risk attached to the proposal is within the limits acceptable to the company, the proposal is accepted. Then the underwriter decides the category in which the risk falls and premium to be paid is calculated accordingly. In the underwriting process, the life insurance agent gives the details of information required by the underwriter.

ENTERING THE PROPOSAL IN PROPOSAL REGISTER

When the proposal is consistent with the rules and the company decides to accept the proposal it is serially numbered and entered in the Proposal Register and Review Slip is made. For every proposal a different file is made containing review slip and other particulars related to the proposal.

SENDING ACCEPTANCE LETTER

The acceptance letter is sent by the insurance company to the proposer. The reminder of the payment of the premium due is also sent to the insured from time to time by the insurance company.

ISSUE OF FIRST PREMIUM RECEIPT

After the acceptance of proposal and payment of premium by the proposer, the insurance company will send First Premium Receipt to the proposer.

POLICY WRITING

The policy is usually written in a special department whose main task is to issue written contracts in accordance with the instructions from the underwriting department.

They also keep a register of policies for future reference. These days, insurance companies are using computers to keep records of clients, the payment of premium and other particulars.

SERVICING OF POLICY-HOLDERS

Servicing of policy holders include:

(1) Proof of age

(2) Nomination

(3) Assignment

(4) Alteration / Changes

(5) Paid up value & surrender value

PROOF OF AGE

The age of the life assured must be proved either during the period of the policy or after the claim arises, because age is an important factor for calculating at the rate of premium to be charged for a particular policy. The age is generally admitted by the following proofs.

(i) Certified extract from Municipal or other records made at the time of birth.

(ii) Original horoscope prepared at the time of birth. If it is found that the horoscope has been prepared for the specific purpose of proving the assured's age, the same should not be accepted.

(iii) Certificate of school or college records if the age or date of birth is stated therein.

(iv) Certificated extracts from the Service Registers of the reputed employer.

(v) Indemnity Cards issued by the Defence Department for its employees.

(vi) Passport issued by Passport Authority of India

(vii) Marriage certificate in case of Roman Catholics issued by Roman Catholic Church.

Cases where admission of age proof is required necessarily at the time of issue of policy.

The age should be proved at the time of issue of policy where the age of the life assured is below 20 or 50 and above, Children's Deferred Assurance Policies, Annuity Policies and policies issued under Salary Saving Scheme. Proof of age is an important issue for insurer as the older people have higher probability of death than the younger ones. So premium rates are calculated on the basis of age groups. Where the insured is unable to give any of the standard age proofs, the insured may accept the age on the basis of a 'Declaration of age' executed by an elderly relative or friend who has personal knowledge of the assured's date of birth. The declaration is required to be adequately stamped according to the stamp regulations. It must be signed by the declarant in the presence of a Magistrate or an officer empowered to administer oaths.

On submission of an age proof, age admission certificate is issued to the policyholder. In case of any difference in recorded age and actual age, the proposal review slip and policy register sheet are corrected accordingly. In case the actual age proves to be lower the excess of premiums charged from the policyholder will be refunded to him.

ASSIGNMENT AND NOMINATION

The Policyholder should be advised for nomination, if no nomination was effected. When nomination or assignment is effected by a policyholder, it should be scrutinized thoroughly to see whether it was in order or not. If there is any material omission or mistake, it may be returned to the policyholder or the assignee with a covering letter giving instructions as to the corrections to be made in the assignment or nomination.

When a document is sent for correction, reminders should be sent every fortnight until the requirements are complied with. The policyholder should follow the instructions printed on the back of assignment or nomination.

NOMINATION

Nomination is the process of identifying a person to receive the policy money in the event of the death of the Policyholder. Nomination can be done at the beginning of the Policy by giving details of nominee in the proposal form. However, if the nomination is not given at the beginning, the policyholder can give it at a later date. For that purpose a prescribed form is to be filled up and nomination can be endorsed on Policy Bond.

Change in Nomination

Change of nomination can be done by the policy holder any time during the term of the policy and any number of times he wants to. Procedure of nomination is same every time.

Withdrawal of nomination

Nomination can be withdrawn by the policy holder without giving prior notice to the nominee.

Nomination can be done only by a policyholder who has attained majority and on a policy on his life. Under Nomination, the Nominee gets only the right to receive the policy money in the event of the death of the Policyholder.

Death of the Nominee If the nominee dies and the policyholder is still surviving then the nomination would be ineffective. If Nominee dies after the death of the Policyholder but before receiving policy money, then also Nomination becomes ineffective and only the legal heirs of the policyholder can claim money.

Nomination at a later date After the policy is prepared and issued and if no Nomination has been given the assured can give the nomination only by an endorsement on the policy itself. A nomination is not required to be stamped. Nomination in favour of a stranger cannot be given as there is no insurable interest involved in that case. For nomination in favour of wife and children, specific names of wife and children should be given.

Successive Nominee

Where it is mentioned in nomination that the policy money should be paid to "Nominee A failing him to Nominee B whom failing to Nominee C, etc.", such nomination is called successive nomination.

Such nomination would be in favour of one individual in the order mentioned. All such Nomination would mean that if Nominee A were dead at the time in question the Nominee B would take the whole amount and that if both Nominees A and B were then dead then Nominee C would take the whole amount and so on.

A Minor Nominee

In view of the Insurance (Amendment Act) 1950, the Life Assured has the right, where a nominee is a minor, to appoint any person as the Appointee to receive the moneys secured by the policy in the event of the assured's death during minority of the nominee.

The person so appointed will not be a guardian of the minor Nominee's power will be limited to the right to receive the policy money in the event of the assured's death during the minority of the Nominee. The appointment must be a major. The appointment of Appointee must be communicated to the insurance company. So his name can be registered with the company. The appointment can be cancelled or changed by the life assured any time before the maturity of the policy.

ASSIGNMENT

Assignment is a means whereby the right and title under a policy gets transferred from assignor to assignee. Assignor is the policyholder who transfers the title and assignee is the person who gets the title of the policy from the assignor. Assignment can be made either by endorsement on the policy or on a separate paper duly stamped. Assignor must be a major. Assignment must be in writing and assignor's signature along with a witness is required. Notice of assignment should be submitted to the insurer by the assignor. Assignment can be of two types:

1. Absolute Assignment: In which all the rights, title and interest of the assignor in the policy passes on to the assignee without the possibility of cancellation of the same.
2. Conditional Assignment: In which the assignor and the assignee may agree that in case specified event or events happen, the assignment would be cancelled or ineffective in part or as a whole.

Impact of Assignment

In assignment, assignor gives all the rights over the policy to the assignee that becomes the owner of the policy. The assignee has the right to reassign that policy.

In the event of Death of the Assignee

If the assignment is conditional assignment and the assignee dies, the assignment becomes ineffective and all the rights and title of the policy goes back to the life assured if he is alive. If the life assured is not surviving, the benefit goes back to the life assured's nominee. In case of absolute assignment, if the assignee dies, all the rights entitled of the policy are given to legal heirs of the assignee.

Cancellation of Assignment

An assignment once executed cannot be cancelled, however, if an assignee during the term of the policy reassigns the interest and title of the policy to the previous assignor such reassignment will result in cancellation of assignment and the benefits of the policy go back to the original assignor.

Procedures of Assignment

A standard form of Assignment is issued to the policyholder who wants to effect an assignment of his policy. Necessary instructions are there for executing the assignment which is then registered by the insurance company. Points to be checked by the insurance company for affecting assignment:

(1) Check whether the assignment is executed on the Policy or on a separate paper and if it is executed on a separate paper that the paper is adequately stamped. If it is unstamped or inadequately stamped inform the assignor and get it corrected.

(2) Check whether notice of assignment is received from the assignor; if the notice is not received or it is defective, inform the assignor.

(3) Check the signatures of assignor affixed to the assignment and notice with the specimen of his signature in the proposal papers to see that they tally. If the signature differs then for writing letter to the person concerned, inform the assignor.

(4) If the assignment is executed on a separate paper, ensure that the paper should be stamped, in accordance with the stamp regulations.

(5) Check that the data and place of execution on Assignment are mentioned. If they are not mentioned the assignment may be registered, if otherwise in order, but while returning the Assignment to the party concerned he should be asked to have the necessary particulars inserted in the Assignment under the Assignor's.

If the assignment is in order and that the notice there of has been duly received the particulars of assignment must be entered in the space provide for the purpose in the Policy Ledger Sheet under the heading "Nominations and Assignments". Also the appropriate rubber stamp is affixed at the foot of assignment write the date on which the assignment and the notice are received.

ALTERATIONS

After issue of a Policy, the Policy holder desires an alteration in the terms thereof to suit his convenience, e.g., an alteration in the mode of payment of premiums, Plan of Assurance, reduction in the premium-paying period, etc. An alteration may be allowed provided the policy is in force and has not become fully paid up.

It is stated in the prospectus that no alteration from one class of Assurance to another subject to a lower scale of premium is permissible.

However, an alteration from the with profits Limited Payment plan to the with profits Endowment Assurance Plan with premiums payable for a term not exceeding the original premium-paying term will be allowed even if the premium payable on alteration is lower. Alterations from certain Classes of Assurance to certain other Classes are not allowed at all.

Frequently requested alterations by the policyholders are:

(1) Alteration in Name;

(2) Reduction in the Sum Assured;

(3) Adding Double Accident Benefit and Extended Disability Benefit.

(4) Alteration in Class or Term;

(5) Removal of an extra premium;

(6) Alteration in the Mode of Payment of Premiums;

(7) Alteration form Without Profits Plan to With Profits Plan;

(8) Correction in Policies;

No alteration will be permitted within one year of the commencement of the policy, except the few cases like:

(1) Compulsory alterations such as alteration in name, correction in policies, alteration in currency of payment of policy moneys and alterations age proving higher or lower than that stated at the time of proposal.

(2) Requests for addition of Double Accident Benefit, Extended Disability Benefit.

(3) Change in the mode of payment of premium to 'monthly' so as to bring the policy under Salary Saving Scheme or to finance the same from Provident Fund Account.

(4) Conversion of ordinary policies to those issued under Married Women's Property Act, as provided in the Manual on the subject of 'Married Women's Property Act'.

ALTERATION FEE

"Alteration fee" is required in the following cases;

(1) Alteration in the mode of payment whereby there is an increase in the frequency of payment of premium

installments, e.g., alteration from yearly to half-yearly, quarterly or monthly, etc.;

(2) When policyholder wants to add Double Accident Benefit or Extended Disability Benefit after the issue of the Policy and such Benefit is not granted from the commencement;

(3) Reduction in the Sum Assured;

(4) When policyholder wants to add Premium Waiver Benefit under a Child Deferred Annuity policy after its issue and such Benefit is not granted form the commencement.

No fee is required for Alterations of the following types:

(1) Where the alteration should necessarily be made in age of the policyholder, as age stated in the policy is not correct. The age stated in the policy may be understated or overstated.

(2) Where policyholder wants to reduce the frequency of payment of installments of premiums in the year.

(3) Where change or correction is required in the name of the assured, nominee, assignee etc., in the policy.

Loan on Policy

Most of the insurance companies give facility to the policyholders to get loans on Life Insurance policies according to rules. The policyholder can apply for a loan in a prescribed form and has to give policy bond along with the completed form.

The loan amount that the policyholder can get is calculated according to surrender value of the policy at the time of taking the loan. Rate of interest charged on the loan by the insurance company may vary from time to time and may depend upon the rules of the insurance company. For loan the policy should be assigned absolutely in favour of the insurance company.

Repayment of Loan

The life assured can repay the loan either in full or in part anytime during the term of the policy. If the loan is not repaid during the term of the policy, the amount of loan and its interest will be subtracted from the claimed amount on the policy and the balance will be given to the policyholder.

When a loan is granted, it is entered with the particulars in the Policy Register Sheet of the insurance company. When the policyholder repays the loan in full or part, the particulars are entered in the Policy Ledger Sheet. Separate loan bond should be made and given to the policyholder for the purpose of granting more than one loans. However, only one cheque may be issued for all the loans.

Generally, the loans are not allowed for the following policies.

1. Immediate Annuity and Deferred Annuity Policies.
2. Children's Deferred Assurance policies during deferment period.
3. Janata Policies.
4. Where the assured or the assignee is incompetent to contract.
5. Where policies carry conditions or endorsements taking away the right of raising loans from the assured.
6. Policies issued under Married Women's Property Act.
7. Where the policies are lost or damaged.

SURRENDER VALUE

If the insured is unwilling or unable to pay the premium of the policy, he may surrender the policy and ask for its surrender value. Surrender value is the cash value payable by the insurance on voluntary termination of the policy contract by the life assured before the expiry of the term of the policy. Surrender value depends on the type of policy and number of premia paid. A policy can be surrendered only when the premia is paid for the three years.

PAID UP VALUE

When a policyholder wants to terminate the policy, he may convert the same into paid-up policy. In this case, the amount of paid-up value is payable to the insured only after the full term (maturity) of the policy. The option of converting the policy into paid up policy and stop paying the further premiums can be taken only if the policy has been in force for at least two years.

3

FURURE PROSPECTS OF INSURANCE

INTRODUCTION

In addition to life, fire and marine Insurance, several other general types of insurances are available today. The nationalized general insurance companies have also been offering special schemes meant for rural areas such as crop insurance, cattle insurance, insurance for huts, poultry etc. There is also a social security group accident scheme covering weaker sections of the society. Some of these are described below:

Personal Accident Insurance

All of us are exposed to the risk of accident, which is a threat to our financial security, and therefore it is prudent to have adequate personal accident cover to manage this contingency. For handling accident risks, personal accident policy, Janata personal accident policy and Gramin personal accident policies are available in India.

Scope of Cover

Personal accident policy pays compensation to the insured in the event of happening of one or more of the following listed below which may be selected by insured at the time of taking policy:

- On death
- On permanent total and partial disability and
- On temporary total disability

In case of accident death during the policy period, the policy in addition covers funeral expenses of the insured person. Permanent total disablement occurs when an individual is unable to perform his regular duties for the remaining part of his life. Permanent partial disablement may result when a person loses any part of his body due to accident.

When an individual is injured in an accident and as a result he is unable to perform his normal duties for a certain period we can describe it as temporary total disablement. This policy can also be extended to reimburse the medical expenses due to accidents up to 10% of the insured amount or 25% of the claim amount or expenses incurred for treatment of the insured person whichever is less. Personal accident policy does not cover the injuries resulting out of war, self-inflicted injury, diseases or insanity, death due to war operations, attempted suicides, accident in armed forces, aircraft accidents, accidents due to nuclear weapons etc.

Janata personal accident policy is meant for weaker section of the society. Thus premium charged under this policy is comparatively less. Gramin personal accident policy is designed for the rural people in the country. It is a contract of Insurance under which the insurer agrees to pay a specific sum of money to the insured in case of bodily injury by accident and to the heirs of the insured in case of death by accident. A contract of personal accident insurance is not a contract of indemnity and the insurer has to pay a fixed sum of money on the death or total disablement of the insured or provide medical benefits for recovery from the injury.

In case of accidental death during the policy period, the policy in addition covers funeral expenses of the insured person. Permanent total disablement occurs when an individual is unable to perform his regular duties for the remaining part of his life. Permanent partial disablement may result when a person loses any part of his body due to accident. It does not cover the injuries resulting out of war, diseases, attempted suicides etc.

Fidelity Insurance

Under this type of insurance contract the insurer undertakes to compensate the insured against the loss caused by misappropriation of funds or goods or damage to the property caused by his employees.

Such a policy is useful to the employers who fear embezzlement, forgery, fraud and dishonesty on the part of their employees. Under it the insured is required to furnish all material facts about the employees and also to notify any change in the condition of their service. The policy can be taken for specific positions rather than names, e.g., accountant, cashier etc. Blanket cover is also available for entire staff or group of employees.

Burglary Insurance

Such a policy provides protection against loss or damage caused by housebreaking, robbery or theft. It is also known as 'robbery, theft or larceny insurance'. For this purpose a comprehensive policy may be taken or each risk may be separately insured. Full details of the article insured are given in the policy. Insured items include gold and gold ornaments and other assets including household items such as TV, fridge, air conditioner etc. A burglary policy for business premises would provide cover against loss to damage by house breaking and burglary of stock-in-trade, goodsin-transit, cash-in-safe, fixture and fittings etc.

Credit Insurance

Credit insurance policy is taken to cover the loss which may arise due to bad debts or non-payment of dues by the debtors. This insurance is very useful to businessmen who sell goods on credit. It protects them from loss arising out of insolvency of their debtors. In India, Export Credit and Guarantee Corporation (ECGC) provides credit insurance to exporters.

Workmen's Compensation Insurance

In India, Workmen's Compensation Act was passed in 1934 and 1946. According to this act, an employer is required to pay compensation to his workers who receive injuries or contract occupational diseases during the course of their work. An employer may obtain an insurance policy to cover such liability. The premiums are payable usually on the basis of wages. It is also known as 'Employers Liability Insurance'. This policy is essential to every employer who employs 'workmen' as defined under the Workmen's Compensation Act in order to protect himself against the legal liabilities arising out of death or bodily injury to this workman. It also extends coverage through reimbursement of medical, surgical and hospitalization expenses including transportation costs on the payment of additional premium. The National Insurance Company Ltd, United India Insurance Company Ltd, Oriental Insurance Company Ltd, and the New India Assurance Company Ltd offer workmen's compensation policies.

Travel Insurance

Travel insurance covers travel related accidents also. While traveling outside India, individuals face risks such as loss of baggage, accidents involving injuries, illnesses and medical emergencies requiring hospitalization treatment. All this can pose serious consequences to the overseas travellers. A rational person should therefore secure the required coverage before leaving his home country. In India travel insurance has become popular among International travellers. The coverage offered under travel insurance policies in India are as follows

Wedding Insurance

These days, weddings have become quite an expensive and elaborate affair. People do take care to make this once-in-a-lifetime event a memorable one. In case of any postponement or cancellation, there is a certain risk of monetary loss. The wedding insurance package can compensate for the monetary loss. This unique product covers the specific risks related to weddings. This Policy can protect you against certain types of financial losses you may incur in the event of unpredictable situations during the period leading up to and including your wedding day.

The period of insurance will be 24 hours prior to the start of the customary functions or rituals or programmes of events mentioned in the printed invitations till the end of the function or five days from the beginning whichever occurs earlier.

This policy provides cover for expenses actually and already incurred or advances paid in connection with marriage hall, catering, pandit, guests, music parties, photos and videography, loss on cancellation of travel tickets etc. Liability is restricted only when such cancellation arises out of cancellation or postponement of marriage.

The policy does not cover any loss arises when marriage is cancelled or postponed because of dispute between marriage parties, willful negligence and criminal misconduct of the bride, bridegroom or their parents.

Employee State Insurance Scheme

The Employee State Insurance Scheme (ESIS) is an insurance system which provides both the cash and medical benefits. It is managed by the Employee State Insurance Corporation (ESIC), a wholly government-owned enterprise. It was conceived as a compulsory social security benefit for workers in the formal sector. The original legislation creating the scheme allowed it to cover only factories which has been using power and employing 10 or more workers. However, since 1989 the scheme has been expanded, and it now includes all such factories which are not using power and employing 20 or more persons. Mines and plantations are explicitly excluded from coverage under the ESIS Act.

Unemployment Insurance

Unemployment insurance is designed to provide short term protection for regularly employed persons who lose their jobs and who are willing and able to work. Unemployment insurance has several basic objectives:

1) Provide cash income during involuntary unemployment.
2) Help unemployed workers find jobs.
3) Encourage employees to stabilize employment.
4) Help stabilize economy.

Unemployment insurance is a popular concept in developed countries like U.S. where they have well defined laws and regulations. However in India it will take a long time to come.

Personal Liability Insurance

Personal liability insurance provides protection against the legal liability, which arises due to insured's personal acts. The insurance company will pay for legal defense to third party damages or injuries up to policy limit. Except legal liability, which arises due to automobile accidents and professional liability, most other personal acts are covered under personal liability insurance.

The personal liability insurance covers damages caused to properties and injuries to other people due to the negligence of the insured. Under this policy, the insurance company is bound to defend the insured, should the matter go to court of law. It can also settle the matter out of court by negotiating with parties for a settlement within the policy limit. Personal liability policy offers very wide coverage. The following instances of loss, damages or injuries caused by an insured individual come under the purview of personal liability insurance in which coverage will be available up to the policy limit.

- Accidental fire to neighbors house as a result of insured's negligence
- Accidental injury to a third party while playing
- Damaging costly antique accidentally belonging to neighbor
- Injuring another person while riding a bicycle

Summary

We have seen that the entire non-life business has been divided into three segments, namely, Fire, Marine and Miscellaneous insurance. Motor and Health are part of Miscellaneous insurance.

Fire insurance is the protection against a loss suffered by the insured as a result of damage caused by fire to the property covered by the policy. Like any other insurance contract it has to satisfy the essentials of a valid contract. e.g. indemnity, insurable interest, utmost good faith etc. Then we have seen the meaning of fire, different types of fire policies and claim settlement procedure.

In marine insurance, the insurer undertakes to indemnify the insured against the losses incidental to marine adventure. Then we have seen characteristics of general insurance, common to marine insurance. The meaning of marine perils, different marine insurance policies, types of marine insurance and types of losses, Clauses and Warranties are also explained. We have tried to understand how the concept of marine insurance evolves specially in India.

Health insurance is a safeguard against rising medical costs. Different types of health insurance policies have been explained. In India, motor insurance is classified as miscellaneous. It comes under tariff category and it offers policies and coverage at standard premium rate. We have also covered the basic principles of motor insurance, classification of vehicles, risks under motor insurance and claim settlement procedure.

Miscellaneous insurance is a large portfolio and has numerous types of policies floated by different insurance companies. For the purpose of this lesson, miscellaneous insurance has been explained through Personal accident insurance, Fidelity insurance, Burglary insurance, Credit insurance, Travel insurance, Workmen's Compensation insurance, Wedding insurance, Employee State Insurance Scheme, Unemployment Insurance and Personal liability Insurance.

BOOMING SECTOR

The reforms in the insurance sector leading finally to the opening of the insurance sector for private participation have brought in its wake major changes not only in the design of the products available in the market but also the manner in which they are marketed. We have today a host of products coupled with a large number of intermediaries who market them.

The post-liberalized insurance industry panorama in India is witnessing dramatic changes in terms of a slew of latest products and services, new channels of distribution, greater use of I.T. as a service facilitator etc. There is also the phenomenon of noticeable shifts in consumer preferences impacting the product mix being offered by insurers. The market structure dominated by a few stabilized public sector players and the 'new' players in the market (some of whom claim their lineage from established international insurance behemoths) is in a state of flux-in terms of figure out market shares but is full of potential.

Added to these are the rising trends of convergence of financial services, especially in the areas like wealth management and evolution of newer risk management tools, particularly in the context of reinsurance management. Greater attention is also being bestowed on the areas like Agricultural Insurance and risk coverage of export-import trade. Then there is impact of visible socio-economic changes like greater urbanization, greater job mobility, growth of the services industry, weakening of traditional family structure, impact of globalization etc. All in all, interesting things are happening in the Indian insurance scene.

*Insurance undergone rapid and massive changes in all aspects of their business: product and services, sectoral structure, market segmentation, competitive environment.*It is believed that the information sharing has not taken its expected shape in the insurance industry for the purposes of practices, research and education. However, data is one of the most needed ingredients in the insurance business development as well as for research and consultancy. There have been regular efforts by IRDA for collection and sharing of the data and other information of public interest. The industry is facing problems in terms of data review as parliament need to register this beforehand. We believe that progress of the industry should not be constrained by any extraneous conditions in the interest of research and development in the area.

Manpower India today released the Manpower Employment Outlook Survey for the first quarter of 2006 revealing sustained positive hiring intentions of employers in India. India continues to lead all 23 countries surveyed this quarter, with a positive overall Net Employment Outlook of +27%. Even though this figure represents a decrease of 13 percentage points from the fourth quarter of 2005, the employment outlook remains extremely healthy. *For the first time since the Survey was launched in India, the Finance, Insurance and Retail industry sector emerged as the most*

***optimistic** sector for a quarter with a Net Employment Outlook of +32%, surpassing the Services sector.*

Privatization of insurance sector has allowed insurance companies to work in the market by depositing 100 crore rupees in the reserve of government. This has encouraged many overseas insurance companies, having a required amount in their reserve, to open their branch in our country. Introduction of the sector has changed the employment pattern, but people must know how to make profit from it. To be in the global market and have advantage of it, capital and skill as per the demand and knowledge of market is the requirement. It is necessary that institutions, which form a part of this financial system, have internal management, governance and accountability structures, which measure up to the highest standards.

INSURANCE IN INDIA

Life Insurance in India was nationalised by incorporating Life Insurance Corporation (LIC) in 1956. All private life insurance companies at that time were taken over by LIC. In 1993 the Government of Republic of India appointed RN Malhotra Committee to lay down a road map for privatisation of the life insurance sector. While the committee submitted its report in 1994, it took another six years before the enabling legislation was passed in the year 2000, legislation amending the *Insurance Act* of 1938 and legislating the *Insurance Regulatory and Development Authority Act* of 2000.

The same year that the newly appointed insurance regulator-Insurance Regulatory and Development Authority IRDA — started issuing licenses to private life insurers.

List of Life Insurers (as of Sept, 2006)

Apart from Life Insurance Corporation, the public sector **life insurer**, there are 14 other private sector life insurers, most of them joint ventures between Indian groups and global insurance giants.

Life Insurer in Public Sector

1. Life Insurance Corporation of India

Life Insurers in Private Sector

1. Bajaj Allianz Life

Pranav,Surat 1

1. Tata AIG Life
2. ICICI Prudential Life Insurance
3. HDFC Standard Life
4. Birla Sunlife
5. SBI Life Insurance
6. Kotak Mahindra Old Mutual Life Insurance
7. Aviva Life Insurance
8. Reliance Life Insurance Company Limited-Formerly known as AMP Sanmar LIC
9. Metlife India Life Insurance
10. ING Vysya Life Insurance
11. Max Newyork Life Insurance
12. Sahara Life Insurance-Now they are not into business
13. Shriram Life Insurance
14. Bharti AXA Life Insurance Co Ltd

Foreign Direct Investment (FDI) Policy in Insurance Sector

As per the current (Mar 06) FDI norms, foreign participation in an Indian insurance company is restricted to 26.0% of its equity / ordinary share capital. The Union Budget for fiscal 2005 had recommended that the ceiling on foreign holding be increased to 49.0%. However, the matter is still under discussions.

Indian Life Insurance Industry Overview

All life insurance companies in India have to comply with the strict regulations laid out by Insurance Regulatory and Development Authority of India (IRDA). Therefore there is no risk in going in for private insurance players. In terms of being rated for financial strength like international players, only ICICI Prudential is rated by Fitch India at National Insurer Financial Strength Rating of AAA(Ind) with stable outlook indicating the highest claims paying ability rating. Life Insurance Corporation of India (LIC), the state owned behemoth, remains by far the largest player in the market. Among the private sector players, ICICI Prudential Life Insurance(JV between ICICI Bank and Prudential PLC)is the largest followed by Bajaj Allianz Life Insurance Company Limited (JV between Bajaj Group and Allianz).

The private companies are coming out with better products which are more beneficial to the customer. Among such products are the ULIPs or the Unit Linked Investment Plans which offer both life cover as well as scope for savings or investment options as the customer desires.Further, these type of plans are subject to a minimum lock-in period of three years to prevent misuse of the significant tax benefits offered to such plans under the Income Tax Act. Hence, comparison of such products with mutual funds would be erroneous.

Commission / Intermediation Fees

- The maximum commission limits as per statutory provisions are:

Agency commission for retail life insurance business:

- 35-40% for 1st year premium if the premium paying term is more than 20 years

- 25-30% for 1st year premium if the premium paying term is more than 15 years
- 10-15% for 1st year premium if the premium paying term is less than 10 years
- 7.5%-yr 2 and 3rd year and 5%-thereafter for all premium paying terms.

In case of Mutual fund related-Unit linked policies it varies between 1.5% to 60% on the premium paid.

o Agency commission for retail pension policies:

* 7.5% for 1st year premium and 2.5% thereafter

- Maximum broker commission-30%
- Referral fees to banks – Max 55% for regular premium and 10% for single premium. However in any case this fee cannot be more than the agency commission as filed under the product.
- However, the above commission may be further subject to the product wise limits specified by IRDA while approving the product.

LIFE INSURANCE CORPORATION OF INDIA

The Life Insurance Corporation of India (LICI) is the largest life insurance company in India; it is fully owned by the Government of India. It was founded in 1956.

Headquartered in Mumbai, which is considered the financial capital of India, the Life Insurance Corporation of India currently has 8 zonal Offices and 101 divisional offices located in different parts of India, at least 2048 branches located in different cities and towns of India along with satellite Offices attached to about some 50 Branches, and has a network of around one million and 200 thousand agents [1] for soliciting life insurance business from the public. The Oriental Life Insurance Company, the first corporate entity in India offering life insurance cover was established in Calcutta in 1818 by Bipin Behari Dasgupta and others. Europeans in India were its primary target market, and it charged Indians heftier premiums. The Bombay Mutual Life Assurance Society, formed in 1870, was the first native insurance provider. Other insurance companies established in the pre-independence era included

- Bharat Insurance Company (1896)
- United India (1906)
- National Indian (1906)
- National Insurance (1906)
- Co-operative Assurance (1906)
- Hindustan Co-operative (1907)
- Indian Mercantile
- General Assurance
- Swadeshi Life (later Bombay Life)

The first 150 years were marked mostly by turbulent economic conditions. It witnessed, India's First War of Independence, adverse affects of the World War I and World War II on the economy of India, and in between them the period of world wide economic crises triggered by the Great depression. The first half of the 20th century also saw a heightened struggle for India's independence.

The aggregate effect of these events led to a high rate of bankruptcies and liquidation of life insurance companies in India. This had adversely affected the faith of the general public in the utility of obtaining life cover. The LIFE INSURANCE Act and the Provident Fund Act were passed in 1912, providing the first regulatory mechanisms in the Life Insurance industry.

The Indian Insurance Companies Act of 1928 authorized the government to obtain statistical information from companies operating in both life and non-life insurance areas. The subsequent Insurance Act of 1938 brought stricter state control over an industry that had seen several financially unsound ventures fail. A bill was also introduced in the Legislative Assembly in 1944 to nationalize the insurance industry.

NATIONALIZATION

In 1955, parliamentarian Feroze Gandhi raised the matter of insurance fraud by owner's of private insurance companies. In the ensuing investigations, one of India's wealthiest businessmen, Ram Kishan Dalmia, owner of the Times of India newspaper, was sent to prison for two months.

Eventually, the Parliament of India passed the Life Insurance of India Act on 1956-06-19, and the Life Insurance Corporation of India was created on 1956-09-01, by consolidating the life insurance business of 245 private life insurers and other entities offering life insurance services. Nationalization of the life insurance business in India was a result of the Industrial Policy Resolution of 1956, which had created a policy framework for extending state control over at least seventeen sectors of the economy, including the life insurance. The company began operations with 5 zonal offices, 33 divisional offices and 212 branch offices.

Current Status

Over its existence of around 50 years, Life Insurance Corporation of India, which commanded a monopoly of soliciting and selling life insurance in India, created huge surpluses, and contributed around 7 % of India's GDP in 2006.

The Corporation, which started its business with around 300 offices, 5.6 million policies and a corpus of INR 459 million, has grown to 2,048 offices servicing around 180 million policies and a corpus of over INR 3.4 trillion.

The organization now comprises 2048 branches, 100 divisional offices and 8 zonal offices, and employs over 1 million agents. It also operates in 12 other countries, primarily to cater to the needs of Non Resident Indians.

With the change in the India's economic philosophy from the early 1990s, and the subsequent relaxation of state control over several sectors of the economy, the monopolistic position of the Life Insurance Corporation of India was diluted, and it has had to compete with a number of other corporate entities, Indian as well as transnational Life Insurance brands.

In the fiscal year 2006-07 Life Insurance Corporation of India's number of policy holders are said to have crossed a whopping 200 million (fourth in terms of population of the countries of the world)

Subsidiaries

LIC owns the following subsidiaries:

- Life Insurance Corporation of India International: This is a joint venture offshore company promoted by LIC which commenced operations in July, 1989 with the objectives of offering US$ denomimated policies to cater to the insurance needs of NRIs and providing insurance services to holders of LIC policies currently residing in the Gulf. LIC International operates in all GCC countries.
- LIC Nepal: A joint venture company formed in 2001 with the Vishal Group of Industries, Nepal.
- LIC Lanka: A joint venture company formed in 2003 with the Bartleet Group of Companies, Sri Lanka.
- LIC Housing Finance: Incorporated in 19th June 1989, its main objective is to provide long term finance forconstruction or purchase of houses or apartments. It has a Dubai office.

- LICHFL Care Homes: A wholly owned subsidiary of LIC Housing Finance, it builds and operates "Assisted Community Living Centres" for senior citizens.

Technology Usage

The insurance giant opted for internet services for all its subscribers and developed massive networking for own usage and internal governance. While the pros and cons of internal networking remains concealed within the officials and hidden for the common customers, the customer portal somehow fails to satisfy the 21st century customers. Apparently, low bandwidth, unwise web page hyper linking, illogical page set ups, all just contribute to the irritation of common net age customers.

The portal gives opportunity to register any policy to be tagged up with any one. As a matter of fact, if Mr. 'A' knows the policy number and premium value of certain policy 'X' of Mr. 'B,' 'A' can tag up 'X' with his own Profile in LICI portal and get all the details of the policy. Moreover, though the organization is officially known as Life Insurance Corporation of India, abbreviated, LICI, the portal welcomes a customer to LIC. As a result of all these, online payment of premium through the site could not be a popular option for the customers. The site fails to show the details of all its recognized agents in its Agent locator section.

STRUCTURE OF INSURANCE

Today, only one business, which affects all walks of life, is insurance business. That's why insurance industry occupies a very important place among financial services operative in the world. Owing to growing complexity of life, trade and commerce, individuals as well as business firms are turning to insurance to manage various risks. Therefore a proper knowledge of what insurance is and what purpose does it serve to individual or an organisation is therefore necessary.

Insurance is a mechanism that ensures an individual to thrive on adverse consequences by compensating the individual his/her loss financially. Every individual in this world is subject to unforeseen and uncalled for hazards or dangers, which may make him and his family vulnerable. At this place, only insurance helps him not only to survive but also recover his loss and continue his life in a normal manner, which would otherwise be unthinkable.

OBJECTIVES

After going through this lesson you should be able to:

- Explain the meaning of insurance
- Understand the nature and characteristics of insurance
- Discuss the need of getting insured and its benefits to individual and business firms
- Describe the types of insurance and their meaning
- List out the meanings of different terms used in the lesson
- Find out the new insurance products available in the market
- Discuss the historical background and the present state of insurance industry after liberalisation of insurance sector.

Meaning and Nature

The term insurance can be defined in financial as well as in legal terms. The financial definition deals with the funding or financial arrangement of the losses whereas the legal definition deals with provisions relating to legally enforceable contract.

Definition in Financial Sense

Insurance is a financial arrangement, which redistributes the costs of unexpected losses among the members of the pool. The pool is a collection of people facing common risks. All members contribute a fixed amount towards a pool called premium. In exchange for the premium payment, the person gets an assurance that a certain sum of money is to be paid to him on the happening of the event insured against. The assurance is that his loss will be made good. Thus, insurance involves the transfer of loss exposures to an insurance pool and the redistribution of losses among the members of the pool.

Definition in Legal Sense

Insurance can be defined as a contract between two parties by which one party undertakes to make good or indemnify any financial loss suffered by other party, in consideration of a sum of money, on the happening of a specified event e.g. fire, accident or death. We call the party agreeing to pay for the losses the insurer. We call the party whose loss makes the 'insurer' pay the claim the insured. We call the payment insured pays to the insurer the premium. We call the insurance contract a policy. In the end we can sum up that insurance is a transfer of risk from the individual to the group and there is a sharing (pooling) of losses on some equitable basis such that fortuitous losses can be indemnified (paid).

Nature of Insurance

The insurance has the following characteristics, which are observed in case of life, marine, fire and general insurance. Sharing of risk-Insurance is a device to share the financial losses which might befall on an individual or his family on the happening of a specified event. The event may be death in case of life insurance, fire in fire insurance etc. If insured the loss arising from these events will be shared by all insured in the form of premium.

(1) Co-operative device-The most important feature of every insurance plan is the cooperation of large

number of persons who, in effect, agree to share the financial loss arising due to a particular risk which is insured. An insurer would be unable to compensate all losses from his capital. So, by insuring a large number of persons, he is able to pay the amount of loss.

(2) Value of risk-The risk is evaluated before insuring to charge the amount of share of an insured, premium. There are several methods of evaluation of risks. If there is expectation of more risk, higher premium may be charged. So, the probability of loss is calculated at the time of insurance.

(4) Payment at contingency-The payment is made at a certain contingency insured. If the contingency occurs, payment is made. Since the life insurance contract is a contract of certainty, because the contingency, the death or the expiry of term, will certainly occur, the payment is certain.

In other insurance contracts, the contingency is the fire or the marine perils etc., may or may not occur. So, if the contingency occurs, payment is made, otherwise no amount is given to the policy-holder.

(5) Amount of payment-The amount of payment depends upon the value of loss occurred due to the particular insured risk provided insurance is there up to that amount. In life insurance, the purpose is not to make good the financial loss suffered.

The insurer promises to pay a fixed sum on the happening of an event. If the event or the contingency takes place, the payment falls due if the policy is valid and in force at the time of the event.

(6) Large number of insured persons-To spread the loss immediately, smoothly and cheaply, large number of persons should be insured. Large number of persons

or property is insured to lower the cost of insurance and the amount of premium.

(7) Insurance is not a gambling-The insurance serves indirectly to increase the productivity of the community by eliminating worry and increasing initiative. The uncertainty is changed into certainty by insuring property and life because the insurer promises to pay a definite sum at damage or death. From the company's point of view, the life insurance is essentially non-speculative; in fact, no other business operates with greater certainties. From the insured point of view, too, insurance is also the antithesis of gambling. Nothing is more uncertain than life and life insurance offers the only sure method of changing that uncertainty into certainty.

(8) Insurance is not charity-Charity is given without consideration but insurance is not possible without premium. It provides security and safety to an individual and to the security although it is a kind of business because in consideration of premium it guarantees the payment of loss. It is a profession because it provides adequate sources at the time of disasters only by charging a nominal premium for the service.

Purpose and Need

Beside things mentioned by you, let's discuss in detail the purpose and need of insurance. As we all know life is full of uncertainties and insurance is based on uncertainties and if there are no uncertainties about the occurrence of a disaster, the concept of insurance will cease to exist. If we all are able to predict the future dangers correctly then we can take a safeguard action to move out of the danger but problem is that we cannot predict death, disaster and danger. All individuals as well as their tangible and intangible assets are exposed to all types of unforeseen risks. Thus insurance is done against such possible contingencies to save the owner and his family from all sorts of sufferings by making good the losses of the unfortunate few, through the help of the fortunate many, who were exposed to the same risk, but saved from the misfortune.

As insurance is a system of sharing risk that seems to be too great to be borne by one individual we can list out the benefits derived by individual and society from the insurance.

(1) Indemnifies loss-Insurance restores people to their former financial position as if no loss had occurred. It helps them to remain financially secure without running into debt after a loss. It also helps business firms to carry on their normal business operations without interruption even after the loss occurs.

(2) Reduces worry and fear-Insurance helps in reducing anxiety and fear before and after the loss occurs, as it is known that the insurance company will compensate the loss.

(3) Makes available funds for investment-Investments are the base of an economic development and mostly these investments are the result of savings. An insurance company is a major instrument for the mobilisation of the savings of people, which are thereafter canalised into investment for economic growth. Insurance provides the continuity in trade and commerce, by covering the risks that could retard the economy and thereby indirectly helps the economy to grow.

(4) Provides employment to a large number of people-Insurance industry offers regular full time employment to a large number of people in the country. Besides them a number of agents, professionals etc.

are also engaged by the industry to render professional services.

(5) Educates people about loss prevention-Insurance companies also engage themselves in educating people about loss prevention. In our country the GIC has created the loss prevention association of India to promote and propagate loss prevention.

(6) Insurance enhances credit worthiness-Insurance policies are often offered as collateral security for credit as well.

(7) Social benefits-Above all we derive social benefits when people with peaceful minds carry on their operations properly and in a better way. Thus insurance's contribution to the economy as a whole is valuable as it avoids economic hardships to people.

Principles of Insurance

Indemnity

A contract of insurance is a contract of indemnity. Indemnity means that the insured in case of loss against which the policy has been insured, shall be paid the actual amount of loss not exceeding the amount of the policy i.e. he shall be fully indemnified. The purpose of contract of insurance is to place the insured in the same financial position, as he was before the loss. Suppose, a person insured his factory for Rs.20 lakhs against fire, the factory is partially burnt and it is estimated that a sum of Rs.10 lakhs will be required to restore it to the original condition. The insurer is liable to pay Rs.10 lakhs only. The exceptions to the rule are found in Personal Accident policies, Agreed Value policies in marine insurance and Valuables and reinstatement policies in Engineering insurance. These are also contracts of indemnity but by a special application of the principle, the amount of indemnity is decided at the time of entering into the contract itself.

In certain forms of insurance, the principle of indemnity is modified to apply. For example, in marine or fire insurance, sometimes, certain profit margin that would have earned in the absence of the event, is also included in the loss. Under life insurance, the insurer is required to pay the fixed amount in the event of death or on the expiry of the period of the policy.

Thus the contract of life insurance is not insurance as such but it is an assurance. This is due to the reason that life cannot be indemnified i.e. the life of a person cannot be valued in terms of money and therefore the question of compensation of actual loss does not arise. Thus a contract of life insurance is a contract of guarantee.

Utmost Good Faith

The doctrine of utmost good faith applies to all forms of insurance. Both parties of the insurance contract must be of the same mind at the time of contract. There should not be any fraud, non-disclosure or misrepresentation concerning the material facts. An insurance contract is a contract of absolute good faith where both parties of the contract must disclose all the material facts truly and fully as insurance shifts risk from one party to another. As in insurance insured knows more about the risks than the insurer, so there must be utmost good faith and mutual confidence between insured and insurer. For instance, if a person suffers from a serious invisible disease but does not disclose this fact while getting his life insured, the insurance company can avoid the contract.

Similarly the insurer must exercise the same good faith in disclosing the scope of the insurance, which he is prepared to grant. Breach of good faith renders the contract voidable ab initio at the discretion of the aggrieved party. A material fact is a fact which would influence the mind of an insurer in deciding whether he should accept the risk, on what terms and what premium he should charge. The utmost good faith says that all material facts should be disclosed in true and full form. It means that the facts should be disclosed in that form in which they really exist. There should no false statement and no half-truth nor any silence on the material facts. What is a material fact depends upon the circumstances of the particular case.

Insurable Interest

For an insurance contract to be valid, the insured must have an insurable interest in the subject matter of insurance. It means that the insured must have an actual pecuniary interest. The insured must be so situated with regard to the thing insured that he would have benefit by its existence and loss from its destruction. For instance, a person has insurable interest in his life or in the life of the spouse but he has no insurable interest in the life of a stranger.

The owner of a building has absolute insurance interest. If this building is financed by banks then financiers too have their interest in the property but is limited to the extent of their financial commitment only. The insurable interest must exist both at the time of the proposal and at the time of claims but in case of life insurance, insurable interest must exist only when the policy is taken.

The essentials of a valid insurable interest are the following:

(a) There must be a subject matter to be insured.

(b) The insured should have monetary relationship with the subject matter.

(c) The relationship between the insured and the subject matter should be recognised by law i.e. there should not be any illegal relationship between the insured and the subject matter.

(d) The financial relationship between the insured and the subject matter should be such that the insured is financially benefited by its existence or survival and will suffer economic loss at the destruction or death of the subject matter.

The subject matter is life in life insurance, property and goods in property insurance, liability and adventure in general insurance. Insurable interest is essentially a pecuniary interest, no emotional or sentimental loss, like an expectation or an anxiety, could be the ground of the insurable interest.

Proximate Cause

The rule of proximate cause says that the cause of the loss must be proximate or immediate and not remote. If the proximate cause of the loss is a risk insured against, the insured can recover. If the risk insured is the outcome of a remote cause, which is not insured against, then the insurer is not bound to pay compensation. Proximate cause means the active efficient cause that sets in motion a chain of events, which brings about a result, without intervention of any force started and working actively from a new and independent source. That means proximate cause is the cause which in a natural and unbroken series of events is responsible for a loss or damage.

If there is a single cause of the loss, the cause will be proximate cause and if the cause of loss was insured, insurer will have to indemnify the loss. When a loss has been brought about by two or more causes, the question arises as to which is the proximate cause. If the causes occurred in form of chain, they have to be observed seriously. For the policy to cover the loss must have an insured peril must occur in the chain of causation that links the proximate cause with the loss. The proximate cause is not necessarily, the cause that was nearest to the damage either in time or in place, but is rather the cause that was actually responsible for loss.

Subrogation

The doctrine of subrogation is a corollary to the principle of indemnity and applies only to fire and marine insurance.

According to it, when an insured has received full indemnity in respect of his loss, all rights and remedies which he has against third person will pass on to the insurer.

The insurer's right of subrogation arises only when he has paid for the loss and this right extend only to the rights and remedies available to the insured in respect of the thing to which the contract of insurance relates.

If the insured is in a position to recover the loss in full or in part from a third party due to whose negligence the loss may have been occurred, his right of recovery is subrogated (substituted) to the insurer on settlement of the claim. The insurers, thereafter, can recover the claim from the third party or in case the lost property is recovered or the damaged property fetches any value, the insurer will be its owner. Suppose, a house is insured for Rs.2 lakhs against fire, the house is damaged by fire and the insurer pays the full value of Rs.2 lakhs to the insured. Later on the damaged house is sold for Rs.20, 000. The insurer is entitled to receive the sum of Rs.20, 000.

Contribution

When an insured obtains more than one policy on one risk, the principle of contribution comes into play. The aim of contribution is to distribute the actual amount of loss among the different insurers who are liable for the same risk under different policies in respect of the same subject matter.

That means the insured may effect more than policy to cover the same risk, he/she cannot recover in total more than a full indemnity (sum insured). In other words, the right of contribution arises when (a) there are different policies which relate to the same subject matter (b) the policies cover the same peril which caused the loss (c) all the policies are in force at the time of the loss and (d) one of the insurers has paid to the insured more than his share of the loss. However, the principle of contribution does not apply to life insurance.

Mitigation of Loss

In the event of a mishap, the insured must take all possible steps to mitigate or minimise the loss to the subject matter of insurance. He should act in the same manner in which he would have acted in the absence of the insurance cover. This means that it is the duty of the insured to make a reasonable effort and take all available precautions to save the insured property.

Warranties

There are certain conditions and promises in the insurance contract which are called warranties. Warranties which are mentioned in the policy are called express warranties. There are certain warranties which are not mentioned in the policy. These warranties are called implied warranties. Warranties, which are answers to the question, are called affirmative warranties. The warranties fulfilling certain conditions or promises are called promissory warranties.

Warranty is the very important condition in the insurance contract which is to be fulfilled by the insured. On breach of warranty the insurer becomes free from his liability. Therefore insured must have to fulfil the condition and promises during the insurance contract whether it is important or not in connection with the risk. If warranties are not followed, the other party may cancel the contract whether risk has occurred or not. However, when the warranty is declared illegal and there is no reverse effect on the contract, the warranty can be waived.

Types of Insurance

The insurance can be divided from two angles: from business point of view and from the risk point of view.

Business Point of View

The insurance from business point of view can be categorised into:

(1) Life Insurance,

(2) General Insurance, and

(3) Social Insurance.

Life Insurance

Life Insurance is different from other insurance in the sense that the subject matter of insurance is life of human being. The insurer will pay the fixed amount of insurance at the death or at the expiry of certain period. At present, life insurance enjoys maximum scope because each and every person requires the insurance. This insurance provides protection to the family at the premature death or gives adequate amount at the old age when earning capacities are reduced. Types of insurance plans offered in our country:

- Term assurance plans
- Whole life plans
- Endowment assurance plans
- Assurances for children
- Family income policy
- Life annuity Joint life assurance
- Pension plans
- Unit linked plan
- Policy for maintenance of handicapped dependent
- Endowment policies with health insurance benefits

General Insurance

The general insurance includes property insurance, liability insurance and other forms of insurance. Fire and marine insurance comes under property insurance. Liability insurance includes motor, theft, fidelity and machine insurances to a certain extent. The strictest form of liability insurance is fidelity insurance whereby the insurer compensates the loss to the insured when he is under the liability of payment to the third party. Types of insurance policies available are:

- Health insurance
- Medi-claim policy
- Personal accident policy
- Group insurance policy
- Automobile insurance
- Worker's compensation
- Liability insurance
- Aviation insurance
- Business insurance
- Fire insurance policy
- Travel insurance policy

Social Insurance

The social insurance is to provide protection to the weaker sections of the society who are unable to pay the premium for adequate insurance. Pension plan, disability benefits, unemployment benefits, sickness insurance and industrial insurance are the various forms of social insurance.

Risk Point of View

Insurance can be divided into property, liability and other forms of insurance.

Property Insurance

Under the property insurance property of a person is insured against a certain specified risks. The risk may be fire or marine perils, theft of property or goods, damage to property at accident. Examples of this are:

- Home insurance
- Business insurance

- Commercial insurance

Marine Insurance

Marine insurance provides protection against loss of marine perils. The marine perils are collision with rock, or ship attacks by enemies, fire and capture by pirates etc. These perils cause damage, destruction or disappearance of the ship and cargo and non-payment of freight. So, marine insurance insures ship (Hull), cargo and freight. Types of policies are:

- Voyage policies
- Time policies
- Valued policies
- Hull insurance
- Cargo insurance
- Freight insurance

Fire Insurance

Fire insurance covers risks of fire. In the absence of fire insurance, the fire waste will increase not only to the individual but to the society as well. With the help of fire insurance, the losses, arising due to fire are compensated and the society is not losing much. The individual is protected from such losses and his property or business or industry will remain in the same position in which it was before the loss. The fire insurance does not protect only losses but it provides certain consequential losses also. Policies available in this insurance are:

- Consequential loss policy
- Comprehensive policy
- Valued policy
- Valuable policy

- Floating policy
- Average policy

Miscellaneous Insurance

The property, goods, machine, furniture, automobile, valuable goods etc., can be insured against the damage or destruction due to accident or disappearance due to theft. There are different forms of insurances for each type of the said property whereby not only property insurance exists but liability insurance and personal injuries are also insured. Miscellaneous insurance covers:

- Motor
- Disability
- Engineering and aviation risks
- Credit insurance
- Construction risks
- Money insurance
- Burglary and theft insurance
- All risks insurance

Liability Insurance

The general insurance also includes liability insurance whereby the insurer is liable to pay the damage of property or to compensate the loss of personal injury or death. The examples of this type of insurance are fidelity insurance, automobile insurance and machine insurance. Examples are:

- Third party insurance
- Employees insurance
- Reinsurance

Other Forms

Besides the property and liability insurances, there are certain other insurances, which are included under general insurance. The examples of such insures are export credit insurances, state employees insurance, etc. whereby the insurer guarantees to pay certain amount at the happening of certain events. Examples are:

- Fiduciary insurance
- Credit insurance
- Privilege insurance

INSURANCE PRODUCTS AND STATE OF INSURANCE INDUSTRY IN INDIA

Terminology

- *Loss* – Loss means being without something which is previously possessed.
- *Total Loss* – A total loss implies that the subject matter insured is fully destroyed and is totally lost to its owner.
- *Actual Loss* – In actual loss subject matter is completely destroyed or so damaged that it ceases to be a thing of the kind insured like complete destruction of cargo by fire.
- *Constructive total loss* – In case of constructive total loss the ship or cargo insured is not completely destroyed but is so badly damaged that the cost of repair or recovery would be greater than the value of the property saved.
- *Partial loss* – A partial loss occurs when the subject matter is partially destroyed or damaged.
- *General Average* – General average refers to the sacrifice made during extreme circumstances for the safety of the ship and the cargo. This loss has to be borne by all the parties who have an interest in the marine adventure.
- *Particular Average* – Particular average may be defined as a loss arising from damage accidentally

caused by the perils insured against. Such a loss is borne by the underwriter who insured the object damaged.

- *Peril* – A peril is defined as the cause of the loss. Examples of perils include fires, tornadoes, heart attacks and criminal acts. Insurance policies provide financial protection against losses caused by perils.
- *Hazards* – hazards are conditions that increase either the frequency or the severity of losses.
- *Warranties* – A warranty is that by which the assured undertakes that some particular thing shall or shall not be done, or that some conditions shall be fulfilled, or whereby he affirms or negatives the existence of a particular state of facts.
- *Reinsurance* – It is an arrangement whereby an original insurer who has insured a risk insures a part of that risk again with another insurer, that means reinsures a part of the risk in order to diminish his liability.
- *Jettison* – Jettison means voluntary throwing away of the cargo or part of a vessel's equipment for the lightening or relieving the ship for common safety. The aim of the intentional throwing away of the goods or property is to relieve the vessel from some imminent peril.
- *Enemies* – The ships belonging to the enemy may cause loss to the insured and is re-underwritten by the marine policy. This policy extends to all the persons of the enemy country and to their hostile acts provided such acts from part of the enemy actions.
- *Agent*–A licensed person or organization authorized to sell insurance by or on behalf of an insurance company.
- *Broker* – A licensed person or organization paid by you to look for insurance on your behalf

- *Burglary* – Coverage against loss as a result of forced entry into premises.
- *Claim* – Notice to an insurer that under the terms of a policy, a loss maybe covered Disability Insurance-Health insurance that provides income payments to the insured wage earner when income is interrupted or terminated because of illness, sickness, or accident.
- *Grace Period* – A period (usually 31 days) after the premium due date, during which an overdue premium may be paid without penalty. The policy remains in force throughout this period.
- *Material Misrepresentation* – The policyholder / applicant makes a false statement of any material (important) fact on his/her application. For instance, the policyholder provides false information regarding the location where the vehicle is garaged.
- *Policy* – The written contract of insurance.
- *Premium* – The amount of money an insurance company charges for insurance coverage.
- *Underwriting* – The process of selecting applicants for insurance and classifying them according to their degrees of insurability so that the appropriate premium rates may be charged. The process includes rejection of unacceptable risks. Workers Compensation Insurance-Coverage providing four types of benefits (medical care, death, disability, and rehabilitation) for employee job-related injuries or diseases as a matter of right (without regard to fault).

New Insurance Products

Some of the new policies are:

(1) Policies under LIC Mutual Fund – LIC launched its Mutual Fund with promise to the investors to provide high returns along with safety and security of investments. LIC Mutual Fund came up with 5

schemes which provide distinct benefits to various cross sections of investors. The names of scheme are:

- Dhanashree 1989
- Dhan 80 cc(1)
- Dhanavarsha
- Dhanaraksha 1989
- Dhanavridhi 1989

(2) Jeevan Akshay – In return for purchase price paid by the purchaser a monthly pension will be paid during the lifetime of the purchaser of the pension. On the death of the pensioner, the original amount invested by the employee along with an additional bonus will be returned to the nominee or his legal heirs.

(3) Jeevan Dhara – The payment of annuities in respect of policies under Jeevan Dhara has to start one month after the completion of the deferment period.

(4) Jeevan Kishor – Children between the ages of 1(last birthday) and 12(last birthday) are eligible to be proposed for insurance under this plan.

(5) Jeevan Chhaya – Couples having a child of age less than one year can avail of this plan, in order to ensure that an adequate financial provision is made for the higher education of the child. The child should not have completed one year of age on the date of the registration. Either father or mother or each one of them individually can take policies under this plan.

(6) Jeevan Suraksha – This policy enables individuals to provide for retirement income from a chosen date. The policy is with life cover but can be taken without life cover under certain conditions.

(7) Rural insurance – The policies offered under this scheme are:

Personal Insurance

(a) Janta Personal Accident (Individual)

(b) Janta Personal Accident (Group)

(c) Gramin Personal Accident

Property Insurance

(a) Agricultural Pumpset

(b) Animal Driven Carts Insurance

(c) Hut Insurance

(d) Gober Gas Insurance

(e) New Well Insurance

Cattle and Livestock Insurance

(a) Cattle Insurance

(b) Sheep and Goat Insurance

(c) Camel Insurance

(d) Horse Insurance

Poultry Insurance

(a) Duck Insurance

(b) Poultry Insurance Master Policy

(8) Insurance of Species

(9) Package Insurance

(10) Crop Insurance

(11) Medi-claim Hospitalisation and

Domiciliary Hospitalisation Insurance

(12) Overseas Medi-claim Policy

(13) Student's Safety Insurance

(14) Unborn Child Welfare Insurance

(15) Cancer Medical Expenses Policy

(16) Boiler and Pressure Plant Insurance

(17) Machinery Insurance

(18) Cold Storage Insurance

(19) Baggage Insurance

(20) Shopkeeper's Insurance

(21) All Risks Cover Insurance

(22) Social Security Scheme

(23) Wedding Insurance

(24) Kidnap and ransom Insurance

(25) Travel Insurance.

4

THEORY OF INSURANCE

INTRODUCTION

In many arenas insurance does work well. We begin by examining what we might think of as par performance for insurance markets, and then grade various insurance areas on how they do on these criteria.

The principal goal of insurance, as assessed by economists, is to transfer resources from low marginal utility of income states to those where the marginal utility of income is high. If insurance is actuarially fair, this process will continue until the marginal utility of money is constant across states. When unfair, insurance will be partial, and greater the greater is risk aversion.

Insurance is most effective when losses are common enough to be of concern but not frequent enough to be routine. Neither asteroid strikes nor car scratches make for good insurable events. Insurance for routine events requires repeated administrative expense that makes the insurance less valuable; the risk spreading benefits are also low. Insuring extremely rare risks also involves reasonable expense, with little compensating gain. Similarly, transactions costs make it important that risks be relatively well defined, and assessable once they happen. Otherwise, claims assessment and litigation can be exceedingly expensive. For most familiar risks, e.g., a house burning down, we would think this condition would be met. However, the recent experience with the one-or-two incident World Trade Center catastrophe makes it clear that there are important exceptions, even with burning buildings. Such ambiguities are more likely where new classes of risk come into play.

Effective insurance also requires that unobservable actions, i.e., moral hazard, not be too significant. Fortunately, major aspects of non-monetary, uncovered loss often assure that this is the case. Thus, for example, rational drivers are not likely to drive at too high speeds because they are insured, and people are unlikely to smoke because they know that if they get cancer, they will receive treatment. The potential for death and disability in these cases counts at least as heavily as covered losses. Monitorable actions (e.g., determining whether a building is kept in safe condition), and risks due to an external source (e.g., earthquakes) also diminish the moral hazard problem.

These important attributes for effective coverage are generally associated with the demand for insurance. The supply side of insurance also determines significantly how well it works. Two critical questions are how diversifiable the risk is, and whether there is an entity that is capable of bearing it. Most familiar insured risks, e.g., the risk of death, are readily diversified cross-sectionally, since the experiences of members of large pools of insureds are effectively independent. There are, however, many critical risks-e.g., the costs of long-term care-where expected costs for different individuals are strongly correlated; they are so-called aggregate risks. Cross-sectional diversification is not possible with these risks, and other risk-sharing arrangements need to be made.

Concerns about the supply-side may seem misplaced in an industry like insurance, where there are many firms and barriers to entry seem relatively modest. Still, competition in insurance seems far from perfect. As one demonstration of this, consider a fundamental attribute of perfectly competitive markets: the law of one price. In a competitive market, the same good should sell at the same price everywhere.

Medigap is an interesting market to study because the policies that can be offered are absolutely standardized, being set by law. Thus, there are no hidden provisions to account for. Still, the price for insurance varies by a factor of four across companies.

AARP has a uniform price by age, while none of the other insurers do. In a situation where consumer shopped around regularly, this would not occur.

Even businesses find it hard, or seem reluctant, to shop for the best insurance deal. Warren Buffett, one of America's shrewder insurance purveyors, announces periodically in his Berkshire-Hathaway report that he will not be writing various types of business coverage this year because the rates are too low.

Buffett suggests that despite expected losses, his competitors are writing insurance to keep their old customers, expecting these customers to stick with them when prices rise.

His competitors at least think cross-elasticity of demand is low for insurance. We consider a large number of potential individual and business risks, and evaluate them on these criteria, effectively seeing how well they are likely to be spread.

Consumer Risks

We analyze three major consumer risks. The first is mortality. Though death is certain, its timing is not. Family-oriented breadwinners would like to insure against early departure. Thus, we expect term life insurance to be a common asset in non-retirement years. Once retired, the demand should tip to annuities that guard against outliving one's assets.

Mortality risk is a classic case where we expect insurance to perform well. On the individual side, the event is obviously infrequent, so that administrative costs are not too high. The loss is also well defined, and moral hazard is contained.

On the supply-side, it is relatively easy to diversify mortality risk across people, since aggregate death rates are generally fairly stable.

The second risk is to health-more specifically the danger of incurring conditions that are expensive to treat. We divide health risks into two categories. The first is short-term health risks. People have variable health needs in the current years, which conventional health insurance covers. Health risk is somewhat less conductive to insurance than is mortality risk. In part, the need for health care is less ideal. While some health needs are truly random, others are routine, such as an annual physical or well-baby care. The costs of running payments for such services through insurance may be high. In addition, moral hazard is an issue in health care. People may (or may not) take much worse care of themselves when they have health insurance-termed ex ante moral hazard-but they certainly use more care when insured than when uninsured (ex post moral hazard), e.g., come in for minor aches and pains. Health insurance is not run like a contingent claims market. Whatever your health condition, the more you spend, the greater the cost you impose on the insurer.

Some health risks are also long-term. Long-term care expenses provide a salient case. About one-third of the elderly will use nursing home care on a sustained basis, and this care can be expensive-costing upwards of $40,000 per year (National Center for Health Statistics, 2003). Because a lot of the gains from long-term care insurance involve pooling people who die without using a nursing home with those who do, this care needs to be purchased before significant morbidity sets in. Risk about future health type is related to long-term care risk. Health insurance for individuals, or the groups they purchase with, is usually experience rated. Should an individual's health decline, or the health of the average member of the group decline, the premium increases. Thus, one might expect people to want insurance against the risk of becoming high cost in the future (Pauly, Kunreuther, and Hirth, 1995; Cochrane, 1995; Cutler, 1996).

Adverse long-term health events are sufficiently infrequent, but not too much so, that insurance makes a good deal of sense, at least in theory. But these risks challenge conventional insurance in three other ways. As with short-term health insurance, moral hazard is likely to be an issue in long-term insurance: if insured, move grandma to the nursing home. In addition, the loss is poorly defined. When does a person need long-term care, and when is she capable of functioning on her own? What does the appearance of a health event today signal about potential future spending? These information problems undermine the viability of long-term insurance. On the supply-side, there is a substantial concern about diversifying these risks. When future medical costs increase for some people-e.g., because expensive new medical technologies become available-they will increase for others as well. Similarly, if new medical knowledge extends survival at older ages, it will yield such benefits to millions. The unhappy side effect is that a much greater percentage of the population will spend a fair amount of time in nursing homes. Such properties of long-term health risks imply that cross-sectional diversification will not be entirely possible.

The final individual risk that we address is property and casualty risk. People own homes, cars, and consumer durables that may burn, crash or break. Consequently, they may want to insure them. Property and casualty insurance has many attributes that are favorable to insurance coverage. The major exception is moral hazard. One might imagine that people drive faster when they are insured, or take less good care of their house or other durables. Some evidence suggests that this is the case (see Cohen and Dehejia, 2003, for a summary), though the evidence is far weaker than for moral hazard in medical care utilization.

While mortality, health, and property/casualty risk are the major individual risks that we consider, it is important to note that there are other risks we are not discussing. Most people owe money on a house, and face a choice between an ostensibly risky debt payment (an adjustable-rate mortgage) versus a fixed, insured payment (a fixed rate mortgage). However, it is not obvious which form should be preferred, i.e., whether the borrower should protect the bank against interest rate movement, or vice versa. We might analyze this financial choice in the same way as other forms of insurance. People might also like insurance for their human capital, for example to guard against depreciation of their skills-think travel agents--or prolonged unemployment. There is public insurance for some of these risks, via unemployment insurance, workers' compensation, and disability insurance. But many risks, e.g., lost productivity, are insured by no one. Moral hazard is clearly a substantial issue for many of these risks. In the interest of brevity, however, we do not consider the entire range of risks that individuals face.

Business Risks

Many business risks are similar to individual risks. Businesses own property, for example, and there is uncertainty associated with damage to that property. Businesses are also liable for damages if someone is injured on their premises, if they are found to cause health harms, or if their employees are mistreated. As with health risks for individuals, we divide property and casualty risks for businesses into two groups. Short-term risks are the most common type of business risk. They encompass most damage to property, and litigation exposure. Most of these risks involve relatively infrequent events (but not too infrequent) and generally have well-defined losses (the World Trade Center being a notable exception). There may be some moral hazard in these actions, but we suspect it is not too large.

Most, but not all, short-term business risks can be diversified cross-sectionally. The most prominent exception is terrorism risk, where the potential losses are so large that even having a substantial insurance pool does not drive the variability of losses particularly low. As a result, we note ease of diversification as being either favorable or adverse.

Long-term property and casualty risks are those risks that will not be realized for some time. Firms may discover only years later that the chemicals in their product increase cancer risk. In the same fashion, obstetricians may be sued years after a birth for complications that were only realized later. One can think of the liability revolution in the 1970s and 1980s as a bad realization of a long-tailed risk. Once again, this long-tailed risk makes diversification difficult, since new knowledge increasing claims against one business are often correlated with increases in claims against another. Difficulties with diversification are a major problem in many litigation risks.

Firms also face risk about employment decisions. Firms may be sued for sexual harassment, unjust dismissal, or unfair hiring practices. This risk has many of the attributes of long-term property and casualty risk.

The event is not very frequent and is well-defined, but may not be diversifiable cross-sectionally. The same legal changes that make liability for pollution or medical harms greater than are thought also increase the potential losses from employment issues.

Finally, businesses have risky obligations for the pensions and health care of retired workers. Many large firms have defined benefit pension plans-plans that obligate them to a specific payment based on the age of the retiree and number of years of service. Retiree health insurance payments may work the same way. If pension costs rise more rapidly than expected, or a firm's earnings fall substantially, the firm may be unable to meet its pension obligations. Moral hazard is of clear importance in this risk. Firms that are doing poorly will underfund their pensions, knowing that if the firm fails it will not have sufficient assets to pay out its pension liabilities.

Diversification issues are also important, since pension and health costs tend to rise jointly across firms. For this and other reasons (perhaps the political imperative of caring for penurious retirees), pension obligations are generally insured through the public rather than private sector. As with individuals, there are other financial risks that businesses might like to insure.

Using sophisticated financial instruments, businesses can often do this. Companies selling abroad can hedge exchange rate risk, and businesses can insure interest rate risk through appropriate derivative securities. To keep our analysis manageable, we avoid consideration of these financial risks.

Bundling Insurance and Other Services or Attributes

Many products that are officially sold or presented as insurance provide more than just financial protection; they bundle other services with the risk benefits. These additional benefits are important to account for in evaluating the insurance policy. In some arenas, insurance products have integrated backwards into purchasing services, or at least procuring them. This enables insurers to purchase products at substantially reduced rates. Health insurance is the most prominent example.

When insurance is coupled with provision, the combination may have significant advantages in exerting leverage as a buyer. This should not be thought of as exclusively or even predominantly as an insurance product, i.e., as a risk-spreading device. Many insurance products couple insurance with a tax shield. The buildup in whole life insurance is not taxed, for example, making that product an excellent vehicle for saving. Health insurance that pays for routine care costs is also a tax dodge, saving the taxation that would be associated with wage and salary payments. The primary motivation for such policies is not the financial risk per se, but the combination of risk reduction and tax rewards.

Still other insurance programs, especially in the public sector, have a strong redistributional element. Government "insurance" programs, such as Social Security and unemployment insurance, almost always have an intended redistributional role. That is, judged ex ante, some participants are hurt and others helped. But even in the private sphere, we see redistribution at play. Thus, young workers usually subsidize older workers in employer-provided health insurance.

Alas, there is no way to discuss insurance without referring to instruments that work as buyers cooperatives, and insurance that significantly redistributes income. These instruments are not strictly insurance. This caveat should inform our discussion below.

INSURANCE IN PRACTICE-CONSUMER RISKS

In this section, we evaluate how insurance for consumer risks fare in practice. Because we consider a number of risks, our analysis is necessarily impressionistic. We rely on conclusions of detailed research studies where possible, and analysis of aggregate data in many cases. For many types of risk, we conclude that insurance performs substantially less well than is anticipated by theory.

Mortality

As Yaari (1965) first noted, life insurance and annuities cater to mutually exclusive circumstances-living too long and living too short; one would not expect the same person to want both in force at the same time.

In practice, life insurance is very common, and annuitization is very rare. The 2001 Survey of Consumer Finances estimates that two-thirds of families have life insurance, including as many as 90 percent of two-adult families. In total, families have $16 trillion of assets in life insurance (American Council of Life Insurers, 2003). Annuities, by contrast, are owned by only a small share of the population, usually as one option in a retirement plan, e.g., with an IRA rollover. Only 8 percent of the population aged 70 and older has an annuity, compared to 78 percent of that group that has life insurance (Brown, 1999). Annuity reserves total less than $2 trillion.

Without knowing individuals' preferences exactly, despite knowing their assets, earnings and family and health status, we cannot tell what insurance arrangement is optimal for them. A married worker might skip life insurance if he does not value highly the consumption of his non-working spouse. Similarly, a couple may not want an annuity in old age if it is penurious relative to assets, or can deal with a declining consumption stream.

Still, one suspects that such cases are rare, and that large consumption changes individuals might experience due to lives cut short or stretched long are not intended. The research literature takes this perspective in evaluating the adequacy of annuitization and life insurance: it has examined whether these products are purchased in sufficient quantity to minimize consumption changes in the event that bad outcomes are realized. Because of the centrality of life insurance and annuities to debates about social security reform, their use has been considered in detail.

The spread of life insurance is expected and valuable, and important as a source of savings as well as security. Still, two aspects of life insurance have drawn attention as being sub-optimal. The first is the substantial rate of life insurance holdings among the elderly (see Brown, 1999, for a review). Some of the elderly, a group whose children are presumably independent, would rationally want life insurance protection (if pensions depend on the survival of one spouse, for example) but three-quarters is a very high share, and even many elderly without dependents have life insurance.

Some work has focused on the high rate of life insurance coverage among the elderly. One proposed explanation is that social security provides too much annuitization, and people offset that by purchasing life insurance. Brown (1999) finds evidence that this is not the case, however; term life insurance is not more likely to be held by people with larger social security payments. He suggests that other explanations are more important: tax policy that allows for tax-free buildup in whole life insurance or tax-free payment of burial costs; and inertia from purchasing life insurance earlier in life. The exact share attributable to each is not entirely known, but the non-tax explanations such as status quo bias (Samuelson and Zeckhauser, 1988) are surely important. The extent of life insurance during the working years seems broadly appropriate, though concerns linger. In particular, some authors have worried about whether people in their working years are sufficiently insured. Recent studies suggest that too few families have life insurance, and many families that have insurance are underinsured. Bernheim, Forni, Gokhale, and Kotlikoff (1999) use data on family income, assets, and demographic characteristics for people aged 51 to 61 (from the Health and Retirement Survey) to examine the consumption consequences should they die.

They estimate that 30 percent of wives, and 11 percent of husbands, would suffer a consumption decline of 20 percent or more if their spouse passed away, a large enough reduction to rule out the explanation of rational preferences, apart from the joint explanation of little concern for and insufficient bargaining power of the dependent spouse. The shortfall in insurance coverage is more surprising given government tax subsidy to employer-paid premiums, and to investment earnings during the life of a policy.

The extent of underinsurance varies with socioeconomic characteristics. After correcting for income and assets, underinsurance is more common among lower income families, and among couples with very asymmetric earnings (for example, one-earner couples). In the latter families, the death of the higher earning spouse would often pose severe hardships for the surviving spouse. Indeed, work by Bernheim, Carman, Gokhale, and Kotlikoff (2001) suggests that two-thirds of poverty among surviving women and one-third of poverty among surviving men results from a failure to purchase sufficient life insurance.

Adverse selection could explain the underpurchase of insurance among some families, but the literature does not suggest that this is important in life insurance. Cawley and Philipson (1999) document that prices decrease with additional purchases, where adverse selection would imply the reverse. They also find that individual forecasts of mortality probabilities do not help predict purchase of life insurance. Life insurance is also estimated to have very low administrative expense. More likely is that these families are simply not planning adequately for adverse events that may occur: they do not forecast the extent of consumption declines should death occur; life insurance never becomes a conscious decision the family makes; or the male decision-maker does not weigh the utility of his spouse very highly.

Annuitization. The central question about annuities is why so few people purchase them. As noted, less than 10 percent of people aged 70 and older have any private annuity, though essentially all elderly have social security and many elderly have defined benefit pension plans.

The administrative load in annuities provides a partial explanation. Mitchell, Poterba, Warshawsky, and Brown (1999) estimate that the load on annuities is about 15 to 20 percent. About half of that is a result of adverse selection; the remainder is marketing costs, processing costs, and insurer profit.

Still, it does not seem possible to explain the low rate of annuitization, even with these administrative costs. First, the investment returns in annuities are strongly tax favored. Second, risk spreading concerns make annuities worthwhile. In a utility-based simulation model of the annuitization decision, Mitchell et al. estimate that people should be willing to pay an administrative fee of 25 percent to annuitize their assets. That is far above the cost that we see in practice. Conceivably, strong bequest motives could explain low rates of purchase. But annuities would be one way to insure the size of the bequest. The literature has not explored the degree or nature of bequest motivation that could help explain these results. We expect that few could stand up to rational economic scrutiny.

The literature speculates more about 'behavioral' explanations for the low rate of annuitization. Anecdotal evidence suggests that many elderly may not be aware of or understand annuities, and many fewer have priced them (further undercutting the high administrative cost explanation for modest use). Other potential customers may fear paying money to an insurance company only to die shortly thereafter without much return. Along the latter lines is the seemingly inexplicable preference some people have for annuities that guarantee a payment for a certain number of years, even if the annuitant dies before that time.

EXTENDING THE THEORY TO MEET THE PRACTICE OF INSURANCE

Formal insurance arrangements date back at least to ancient Greece. Marine loans in that era advanced money on a ship or cargo. It would be repaid with substantial interest if the voyaged succeeded, but forfeited if the ship was lost, much like the structure of contemporary catastrophe bonds. The interest rate covered both the cost of capital and risk of loss.

Direct insurance of sea risks, using premiums, probably started around 1300 in Belgium. The first known life insurance policy was written in 1583. By the end of the 17 th century, sea risk insurance had evolved to a competitive process between underwriters evaluating risks and meeting at Lloyd's coffee house, the precursor to Lloyds of London.

Today, insurance is a major industry established throughout the world. It moves progressively into new fields. For example, health insurance was virtually unknown in the United States prior to 1929 and now pays for more than 10 percent of the US GDP. Risks ranging from a Camcorder breaking down to being sued for sexual harassment are all insurable events. In recent decades, economic attention has caught up with the remarkable burgeoning of the insurance industry. This is largely attributable to the explosion in attention to information in economics. Indeed, insurance so well fits this attention that it is a major topic of introductory discussions about the role of information in economics. Moreover, the core insurance topics of moral hazard and adverse selection have been transplanted to fields like labor economics and finance.

This sounds like a happy confluence of theory and practice growing up alongside one another: theory improves by studying practice, and practice draws on the results of theory. A principal theme of this essay is that perception is fundamentally wrong. We believe that there is an increasing divergence between the theory of insurance and insurance practice. Consider the following quiz about optimal insurance.

1. Suppose that a risk goes from negligible to possible--for example, the increased probability of a terrorist

accident on US soil after September 11, 2001. Would you expect the private market to provide (a) more insurance; or (b) less insurance?

2. A 70 year-old unmarried woman has three children, all of whom are comfortably middle class. Would you expect her to be more likely to hold (a) an annuity; or (b) life insurance?
3. A consumer buys a $620 camcorder and is offered insurance in case it breaks. The insurance is for three years and costs $120, supplementing the 1 year parts and labor that comes with the camcorder. The probability of a camcorder needing a repair over three years is 8 percent (mostly in the first year), with average repair costs of $125. Would you expect the person to (a) decline the insurance; or (b) accept the insurance.

In each case, optimal insurance principles suggest that (a) is the right answer. But (b) is the answer we often see in the world. Coverage for terrorism risk plummeted after the attacks in September 2001, despite the greater demand for care. About seven times more elderly people have life insurance than annuities, in spite the fact that incomes of children are rising over time.

And insurance against small cost consumer durables is among the most profitable items sold by commercial electronics stores. For almost all products, one in five of the customers purchase it; for some it is four in five. We argue in this paper that these examples are not minor anomalies, but reflect a systematic tendency for insurance in practice to differ from insurance in theory. We discuss and grade a number of insurance settings: mortality, health, and property risk for individuals; and property, liability, environmental, and terrorism risk for businesses. In the vast majority of cases, we argue that insurance in practice diverges from insurance in theory.

The divergence is of two forms. First, insurance is often purchased-sometimes at excessive prices--when theory would suggest it should not, and many significant risks that should be insured are not. The case of life insurance among the elderly, or insurance for minor consumer durables, is an example of the former. The lack of coverage for terrorism insurance is an example of the latter. Second, there are significant mismatches between parties who should bear risk and those who actually do. Risks can be borne by public entities, private (for profit and not-for-profit) firms, and through financial markets. In practice, the allocation of risk across these entities seems suboptimal. Governments insure risks that the private sector might better bear, and financial markets, with their vast resources and wide participation, are not the risk bearer for many large private risks.

The divergence between theory and practice is not a result of moral hazard or adverse selection. In many settings with failures, information is as close to symmetric as it is possible to be, and moral hazard is extremely implausible. Rather, we argue that the divergence of insurance theory and practice is a result of three phenomena, the first on the supply side, the second on the demand side, and the third a true joint product. The first is highly incomplete diversification on the part of insurers. This outcome, we believe, arises due to contracting problems on the supply side of insurance. Investors in insurance companies may be nearly risk neutral for virtually all insurance decisions, but managers of insurance companies are not. Risks that are hard to predict, or are correlated across insureds, may result in the insurance company losing significant amounts of money, with some people being blamed and losing their jobs. We argue that this is an important reason why large but nontraditional risks, e.g., terrorism or long-term health care, are not insured.

Contracting difficulties also help explain why financial markets, with assets in the trillions, as opposed to billions for insurance companies, have not played a more significant role in insurance. One challenge is to secure collateral from investors-the ideal source to cover claims-in case a claim arises. Catastrophe bonds are a small step in this direction, but there is no reason to use as collateral only fixed-income investments. In time, we expect, individuals will be able to participate in insurance pools by pledging such assets as stocks and real estate. A second challenge is to marry insurance expertise with ready pools of capital. Such marriages have been highly successful in such areas as venture capital and hedge funds.

The standard financial arrangement for such contracts (a management fee and a share of profits) may not be sufficient, though, since profits on insurance may be large until an adverse event occurs. Still, there is plenty of money to write insurance, and ample expertise to write the insurance effectively, even if bringing the two together will require innovative institutions and creative contracts.

The demand side contributes its share to the poor performance of insurance relative to theoretical par. The central problem is that people have severe difficulties making decisions where small probabilities and significant stakes are involved. These difficulties have been discussed in the burgeoning literature on behavioral economics and behavioral decision-making, which was pioneered by Amos Tversky and Daniel Kahneman, and for which Kahneman shared the 2002 Nobel Memorial Prize in Economics. People seem (irrationally) fearful of uninsured losses. They overly project their unhappiness and regret were a bad event to occur, and they misjudge probabilities. As a result, people often insure when theory would say they shouldn't; they insure against small risks; they take deductibles that are way too small; and they insure against events that though tragic do not change the marginal utility of income.

The third problem is what we refer to as probability monopoly. It arises when sellers of insurance know risks much better than buyers, and when there is limited competition. Sellers then set prices well above actuarial and administrative cost so as to capitalize on potential buyers' misestimates. Buyers that overestimate the risk of breakdown purchase insurance, at a profit for the insurer.

In the remainder of the paper, we develop these themes about the operation of insurance markets in theory and practice. We introduce areas where we think the theory of insurance should be extended if it is to explain practice, such as understanding what benefits actual purchasers believe they get when they purchase insurance. We start with some basics on when we expect insurance to be widespread, and then turn to an evaluation of insurance markets in practice.

We note at the outset that this is a thought piece. Thus, it tries to present neither rigorous theory nor detailed empirical analysis. It draws data from many sources and arenas to illustrate its themes. And it is speculative in part to be provocative. Thus, for example, we provide our own grades for the functioning of insurance markets across many areas.

THE REBALANCING BONUS: THEORY AND PRACTICE

Let's assume that you have decided that your desired portfolio composition consists of 50% S&P 500 stocks and 50% long term US treasury bonds. (If you've gotten this far in this website you probably already know that this is a fairly undesirable mix; it merely serves as a good example.) As these two assets frequently move in different directions, the portfolio will eventually drift from the desired 50/50 mix. If you desire to maintain the 50/50 composition, some of the better performing asset must be sold, and exchanged for a similar amount of the more poorly performing asset. This is known as portfolio rebalancing. An understanding of the mechanics of rebalancing is fundamental to sound portfolio management, and yet surprisingly little theoretical attention has been paid to this area. Three important questions concerning rebalancing arise:

1. Should rebalancing be done at fixed regular intervals ("periodically"), versus whenever the asset mix gets out of kilter by a certain amount ("threshold rebalancing")?
2. If done periodically, what is is the optimum interval (i.e., monthly versus quarterly versus annually)?
3. Is there a way to predict how much extra return is available from rebalancing, and is it possible to identify assets which provide superior rebalancing benefit?

For example, Markowitz1 considers the return of a portfolio to be equal to the weighted sums of the individual component returns, but this formulation is valid only for nonrebalanced portfolios over single periods. It is surprising that Markowitz considered portfolio return to be the weighted sum of the component returns, since he pioneered the idea that portfolio variance, or risk, is not the weighted sum of the individual component variances. In Portfclio Selection he presented Monte Carlo simulations in which the actual returns were significantly higher than the arithmetically derived expected returns, but did not comment on the discrepancy.

A simple, well known example will suffice: The return on common stock for the period 1926-94 was 10.19%, and for long term corporate bonds over the same period 5.51%.5 The "Markowitz return" on an equal mixture of the two is the arithmetic mean, or 7.85%. Rebalancing this portfolio on an annual basis to maintain a 50/50 mixture yields a return of 8.34%; a "rebalancing bonus" of 0.49% is realized over the Markowitz return. In fact, however, if one had put equal amounts of money into stocks and bonds on January 1, 1926, and had not rebalanced or paid taxes, then the long term return would have been 9.17%. In this instance the nonrebalanced portfolio has a higher return than the rebalanced portfolio. This is because over the 69 year period studied the significantly higher stock return overwhelms the bond return; for the last 40 years of the period the unrebalanced portfolio consists of greater than 90% stock.

Thus the higher return of the unrebalanced portfolio comes at the cost of a much higher risk than the rebalanced one. Perold and Sharpe2 point out that rebalancing is a "concave" strategy. Portfolio insurance represents the opposite of rebalancing, and is referred to as a "convex" strategy. They suggest that convex portfolio insurance strategies as well as buy and hold ("flat") strategies produce superior returns in markets with a prolonged upward (or downward) bias, and concave rebalancing strategies produce superior returns in stagnant markets. If the only two assets considered are stocks and bonds, and if stock returns are always higher than bond returns over long time horizons, then obviously buy and hold, as well as portfolio insurance, will produce returns superior to rebalancing.

As already pointed out, this will come at the cost of gradually increasing portfolio risk. However, things are very different when looking at global equity portfolios. Over very long time horizons there is usually relatively little difference in the returns in most national equity markets; under such circumstances rebalanced portfolios dominate. For example, when looking at the 1970-94 period, rebalancing various asset pairs almost always provides returns superior to nonrebalanced porfolios. Only when long term return differences among asssets exceed 5 percent do nonrebalanced portfolios provide superior returns, and then only at the cost of increased risk. (The exceptions which prove the rule are the very high returns of Japanese equity, and the very low returns of Australian and Italian equity.)

Care should be taken to note that the superiority of rebalancing as a long term strategy pertains only to national and regional markets as a whole, and not among different industry groups. Over the course of decades entire industries often shrivel while others prosper mightily; rebalancing the pharmacutecal and petroleum segments of the S&P500 over the past three decades would have been a disastrous strategy. Although enitre national markets occasionally disappear throught war or nationalization, this occcurs much less frequently than the ongoing remolding of market segment capitalization characteristic of a market economy.

ESTIMATING THE REBALANCING BONUS

A small thought experiment is in order. Let us postulate a portfolio composed of equal parts of two assets, A and B. Further assume that each has a return of either +30% or-10%, with equal probability, and that the portfolio is rebalanced to 50/50 at the end of each year. The long term return of each asset is 8.1665% when annually compounded, and its standard deviation 20%. If the annual returns are perfectly correlated (i.e., r =1) then the equal mixture of A and B will have the same risk and return as each individual asset, and no gain in risk or return is obtained by diversification. Now assume that there is a zero correlation between the returns of A and B. This can be symbolically represented by returns for four periods:

Case 1

Asset	Year 1	Year 2	Year 3	Year 4
A	+30	+30	-10	-10
B	+30	-10	+30	-10
Equal Mix	+30	+10	+10	-10

This example yields an annualized return of 9.0794%, and a standard deviation of 14.142%. The standard deviation of the portfolio has been reduced by a factor of the square root of 2 (and the variance halved) as predicted by Markowitz. However, the return is 0.9129% higher than the Markowitz return. Further, this excess return would not have been realized without rebalancing. This portfolio thus has a "rebalancing bonus" (hereafter known as the "RB") of 0.9129%. If instead the returns on A and B are perfectly inversely correlated (r =-1) it can be seen that the return of the portfolio each year will be 10%, as will be the annualized return, and the standard deviation and variance zero. The RB will thus be 1.8355% in this highly theoretical instance, which is slightly more than twice the bonus in the instance where r =0. Simple inspection suggests that the RB is proportional to:

(1-correlation coefficient)

Assume that the returns on asset A are still +30 and-10, but that now the return on B can be either +15 or +5. Asset B then has an expected return of 9.8863%(and a standard deviation of 10%; one half of the SD of asset A). The Markowitz return for a 50/50 mixture of A and B is 9.0264% (the average of 8.1665% and 9.8863%).

For the r =0 uncorrelated example:

Case 2

Asset	Year 1	Year 2	Year 3	Year 4
A	+30	+30	-10	-10
B	+15	+5	+15	+5
Equal Mix	+22.5	+17.5	+2.5	-2.5

Here, the annualized return is 9.5155%, yielding an RB of 0.4891%, or about one half of the uncorrelated example in case 1. Further experimentation demonstrates that the rebalancing bonus of any combination of two assets is roughly approximated by the expression:

X1X2SD1SD2(1-correlation coefficient)

where SD1 is the standard deviation of asset 1, X1 is the amount of asset 1.

Taking this process one step further, consider the case where an asset with returns of either +30 or-10 is mixed with a riskless asset whose return is always zero. The return on a 50/50 mix of these two assets will be either +15 or-5. The Markowitz return of this mix is 4.0833% (the mean of 8.1665 and zero), but it's actual return is 4.5227%, yielding an RB of 0.4394%. Since the standard deviation of the riskless asset is zero, the expression derived above will equal zero also, so an additional term is needed. A bit more experimentation shows that this term can be closely approximated by:

X1X2(SD1-SD2)2/2

Thus, it is postulated that the "theoretical RB," RB1,2, can be expressed as:

RB1,2 = X1X2{SD1SD2(1-C.C.) + (SD1-SD2)2/2}

or more simply,

X1X2(Var1/2 + Var2/2-Covar1,2)

Stated succinctly, the intrinsic rebalancing potential of any asset pair is the difference between its mean variance and covariance. The above formulation was tested for 50/50 mixtures of asset pairs of the below assets:

S&P 500 index

MCSI-EAFE

US 9-10 portfolio (DFA US small co. portfolio)

Equity REIT(NAREIT index)

MSCI-EAFE Europe

MSCI-EAFE Pacific

MSCI-EAFE Emerging Markets

UK small stocks(DFA UK small co. portfolio)

Japanese small stocks(DFA Japanese small co. portfolio)

Continental European small stocks(DFA Continental small co. portfolio)

Precious Metals(Morningstar fund index)

Natural Resources(Morningstar fund index)

Lehman Long Term Government Index

International Bond(Morningstar fund index)

One year corporate notes(DFA one year fixed fund)

The theoretical RB was calculated from SDs and correlation coefficients derived from quarterly data for the period July 1988 to December 1994. Similarly, the "actual" portfolios were rebalanced quarterly. A linear correction was applied to each series of quarterly returns to yield a zero annualized return for each individual asset over the whole study period; thus any return obtained from the asset pair must be due to rebalancing. The 105 resultant theoretical/ actual data points for each asset pair were plotted in Figure 1. As is seen, the theoretical data is highly predictive of the actual data, with an R2 of 0.983 and a standard error of 0.052% of yield.

To summarize thus far: The beneficial effect of poorly correlated assets on portfolio risk, undoubtedly appreciated since antiquity, was mathematically formalized only forty years ago by Markowitz. The above theoretical model and backtested portfolios suggest that significant excess return is available from combinations of asset pairs which have both low correlation and high risk.

The capital asset pricing model asserts that the "risky" portion of one's portfolio should be a capitalization weighted "market portfolio" of all the world's investible risky assets.3 The above considerations provide an argument against portfolio capitalization weighting, since by definition capitalization weighting denies the need for rebalancing. Assets and sectors which have been battered or inflated will find their capitalization weighting commensurately reduced or increased. Consider the MSCI-EAFE index. During the study period July 1988 to December 1994 the US investor passively employing this index saw their percentage of Japanese holdings increase and decrease precipitously.

On the other hand, the investor who kept his or her foreign assets equally divided between the European and Pacific sides of this index reaped an excess return of 0.588% for the period studied, with a modest concomitant reduction in risk. The emerging markets provide an even more vivid example of this phenomenon. The Latin American and Far Eastern components of the MSCI-EAFE EM index have very high standard deviations and are imperfectly correlated. The above model suggests that the investor who actively rebalances these two sectors will reap an advantage of at least two or three percent over their passively invested colleague. It seems highly likely that adherence to fixed percentage allocations among finely divided market sectors offers significant advantages over a passive market portfolio/ market capitalization approach.

FREQUENCY OF REBALANCING

Although the need for portfolio rebalancing to policy composition is generally acknowledged, scant attention has been paid to it's frequency. In a rare paper addressing this issue, Arnott and Lovell 4 found that for the years 1968-91 a 50/50 stock/bond mix produced a return of 9.02% for annual rebalancing, 9.12% for quarterly rebalancing, and 9.16% for monthly rebalancing. Trading costs reduced the rebalancing benefit slightly, but even monthly rebalancing was still of benefit after transaction costs were considered. They also found that nonperiodic "threshold rebalancing" when portfolio composition surpassed 1%, 2%, and 5% excess/deficiency produced somewhat lesser gains. They surmised "Over this period, regular monthly rebalancing returns dominated less active approaches. Should one infer that daily rebalancing is better still? One cannot say, but it seems plausible."

The above formulation provides a framework for further investigation of the rebalancing frequency problem. One can calculate a "theoretical rebalancing bonus" for each of the different periods. It is well known that asset return correlations vary somewhat over time. It is less well appreciated that the individual return standard deviations and paired correlation coefficients are not the same for differing sampling intervals within the same epoch. For a given historical epoch the standard deviation of returns of a single asset may be different for shorter or longer measuring intervals. Even larger differences may be present for correlation coefficients of asset pairs.

To illustrate this point, and to provide a basis for further discussion, I have provided standard deviation and correlation data for five different assets for monthly, quarterly, and annual returns in Table 1: UK, Japanese, Continental, and US 9-10 decile small stocks, and the MSCI-Emerging Markets Index, again for the July 1988-December 1994 period. These particular assets were chosen because of their low mutual correlations and high return standard deviations.

(m=monthly, q=quarterly, a=annual All SDs are annualized, calculated as twice the quaterly SD, and 3.4641 times the monthly SD)

Next, "actual" or "observed" RBs for the resultant 10 asset pairs were calculated for monthly, quarterly, and annual rebalancing, and compared to the "theoretical," or "predicted" value. The data are presented in Table 2.

These data make three main points:

(1) No one rebalancing period dominates. Monthly rebalancing was best in three cases, quarterly in four, and annual in three.

(2) The theoretical RB was highly predictive in all cases where significantly different rebalancing bonuses were obtained with different intervals. Only in three instances were minor (<0.05%) ranking errors made. Further, in cases where significant advantage is gained

by the use of a particular rebalancing period complex calculations are not necessary. For example, it can be seen that for the pair Jap./EM, quarterly rebalancing is clearly superior to monthly or annual rebalancing.

(3) Those who rely on optimization procedures must be cognizant of the sampling interval used to calculate the standard deviation and correlation input data. Optimization outputs are liable to be very different for data obtained from monthly, quaterly, and annual sampling from within the same historical period.

Obviously, real portfolios are far more complex than asset pairs. It seems reasonable to assume that, analogous to the Markowitz formula for portfolio variance, the formula for a portfolio RB can be represented by:

½(SUMi=1..n)(SUMj=1..n)RBij

(Each term for which i=j will be zero.) Applying this formula to an equal mix (20% each) of the five assets used above yields an observed/predicted RB of 1.205/1.118% for annual, 1.542/1.556% for quarterly, and 1.304/1.301% for monthly rebalancing.

The annualized portfolio SDs are 16.80% for annual, 13.65% for quarterly, and 14.55% for monthly rebalancing--the same preference ranking as for the RB. This should not be surprising as asset pair covariance is the dominant component for both portfolio RB and portfolio variance for porfolios where n>2.

Further work is necessary to evaluate the value of this formula for the estimation of rebalancing benefit for more complex portfolios. It may transpire that the complex relationship between pair correlations and single asset standard deviations measured over shorter or longer time period lengths will not be stable enough to render ex post analysis of much value.

PRECIOUS METALS STOCKS–A SPECIAL CASE

The portfolio characteristics of precious metals equity are unique; very low long term return, very high return variance, and near zero correlation with most other asset classes. One of the primary rationales for this behavior is that most of the risk of this asset class is nonsystematic because of its low correlation with other assets--in other words, it can be diversified away. The above discussion provides another perspective on this paradox. Examination of the theoretical rebalancing formula shows that the addition of a small amount of a high variance zero correlating asset to a portfolio with a much lower variance increases its apparent return by approximately one half of its variance.

In other words, since the variance of a typical portfolio of precious metals stocks is about 0.1, its apparent return (IRR) in a rebalanced portfolio will be about 5% higher than its long term stand alone return. This is precisely what is observed by the investor who periodically rebalances the precious metals component of their portfolio as a fixed proportion; a large fraction of the IRR of this component comes from rebalancing per se. Thus, not only is the systematic risk of precioius metals stocks much lower than its stand alone risk, but its rebalanced portfolio return is much higher than its observed stand alone long term return.

CONCLUSIONS

1. The expected return of a rebalanced portfolio is not accurately represented by simple arithmetic weighting of individual asset returns. This is particularly true of assets which have high standard deviations and are poorly correlated. This may be of some importance to those utilizing optimization technology which depends on linear expected return determinations. Standard MVO techniques underestimate the benefit of high variance/low correlation assets.

2. The capitalization weighting suggested by the CAPM does not appear to be maximally efficient.
3. A formula is presented which accurately predicts rebalancing benefit. The inputs to this equation are portfolio composition, individual asset standard deviation/variance, and asset pair correlation/ covariance. Since these parameters vary with sampling interval, it may be possible to use this formula to predict the optimal rebalancing frequency. Further, the results of the analyses presented suggest that shorter rebalancing intervals may not always be optimal.
4. Optimizers should understand that sampling interval will significantly affect both input and output data, and that he or she is optimizing only for standard deviatons (or other risk measures, such as semivariance) over a given sampling interval.

SUMMARY

As a means of keeping track of the evidence, we provide our net assessment of the various insurance markets we consider. To keep the analysis simple, we use a three-point scale: good, fair, or poor. We recognize that this assessment is highly subjective; readers may take issue with particular values, or even the scale that we use. On the basis of the evidence, we grade life insurance as fair and annuities as poor. Life insurance earns a higher grade because it functions well for many people. But in both cases, there is some underinsurance, and in the case of life insurance some overinsurance as well.

5

PRESENT STATUS OF INSURANCE

INTRODUCTION

The insurance industry in India can be discussed in two ways – its historical background and its present state. Insurance in India is nothing new. It had its origins in the early 19th century with the arrival of British enterprise in India. Insurance, particularly non-life remained an urban oriented activity of the Insurance companies operating through their agencies. The Life Insurance Corporation of India (LIC) came into existence by an Act of Parliament, viz. LIC act, 1956, with a capital contribution of Rs.5 Crores from the Government of India General Insurance Corporation Of India-The General insurance business in India started with the establishment of Triton Insurance Company Limited in 1850 at Calcutta.In 1907, the first company, The Mercantile Insurance Ltd. Was set up to transact all classes of general insurance business. General Insurance Council, a wing of the Insurance Association of India in 1957, framed a code of conduct for ensuring fair conduct and sound business practices. In 1968 the Insurance Act was amended to regulate investments and to set minimum solvency margins. In the same year the Tariff Advisory Committee was also set up. In 1972, The General Insurance Business (Nationalisation) Act was passed to nationalise the general insurance business in India with effect from 1st January 1973. For these 107 insurers was amalgamated and grouped into four company's viz., the National Insurance Company Ltd., the New India Assurance Company Ltd., the Oriental Insurance Company Ltd. And the United India Insurance Company Ltd. General Insurance Corporation of India was incorporated as a company.

Current Scenario

In new economic policies formulated since 1991, globalisation, privatisation and liberalisation have become new buzzwords. Under new economic policies, many economic and financial reforms took place. Like liberalising licensing policy, attracting FDI, allowing foreign equity in public sector undertakings. The financial reforms restructured banking sector by allowing entry of new private and foreign banks. They also allowed private sector and commercial banks in mutual funds investment business, rationalising the EXIM policy and so on.

Insurance Sector Reforms

After the nationalisation of the life insurance industry in 1956 and the general insurance industry in 1972, the insurance industry confined only to the operations of LIC, GIC and its four subsidiaries viz. The National Insurance Company Limited, New India Assurance Company Limited, Oriental Fire and General Insurance Company Limited and United India Fire and General Insurance Company Limited. Over the years this state monopoly resulted in complacency, use of outdated technologies, inefficient and insufficient customer services and non-coverage of the potential market. Recognising this, the Government set-up a high-powered committee headed by Mr. R. N. Malhotra.

Malhotra Committee

Purpose

In 1993, Malhotra Committee, headed by former Finance Secretary and RBI Governor, was formed to evaluate the

Indian Insurance Industry and recommend its future direction. The committee was set up with an objective of complementing the reforms in the Indian Financial sector. The reforms were aimed at "creating a more efficient and competitive financial system suitable for the requirements of the economy keeping in mind the structural changes currently underway and recognising that insurance is an important part of the overall financial system where it was necessary to address the need for similar reforms." Besides this, the Malhotra committee was asked to make recommendations for changing the structure of insurance industry, to make specific suggestions about how to improve the functioning of LIC and GIC and to recommend on regulation and supervision of the insurance sector in India. Besides this, the committee was asked to assess the strengths and weaknesses of the existing insurance industry and to make recommendations for changes in its functioning and the general policy framework keeping in mind the reforms under way in other parts of the financial sector.

Recommendations

In 1994, the committee submitted the report and gave the following recommendations:

Structure

- Government stake in the insurance companies to be brought down to 50%
- Government should take over the holdings of GIC and its subsidiaries so that these subsidiaries can act as independent corporations
- All the insurance companies should be given greater freedom to operate.

Competition

- Entry of private sector companies within well defined parameters of nature of business.

- Private Companies with a minimum paid up capital of Rs.1 billion should be allowed to enter the industry
- No Company should deal in both Life and General Insurance through a single entity
- Selective entry of foreign insurance companies preferably through joint ventures.
- Postal Life Insurance should be allowed to operate in the rural market
- Only one State Level Life Insurance Company should be allowed to operate in each state
- The insurance Act should be changed
- Controller of Insurance should be made independent
- Establishment of a strong and effective Insurance Regulatory Authority (IRA) as a statutory autonomous board.

Investments

- Mandatory Investments of LIC Life Fund in government securities to be reduced from 75% to 50%
- GIC and its subsidiaries are not to hold more than 5% in any company

Customer Service

- LIC should pay interest on delays in payments beyond 30 days
- Insurance companies must be encouraged to set up unit linked pension plans
- Computerisation of operations and updating of technology to be carried out in the insurance industry Overall, the committee strongly felt that in order to improve the customer services and increase the coverage of the insurance industry should be opened up to competition. But at the same time, the committee

felt the need to exercise caution as any failure on the part of new players could ruin the public confidence in the industry. The recommendations of the committee were discussed at different forums. The recommendations to set up an autonomous IRA found wide support. Since enacting legislation for creating the statutory IRA was to take time, the then government constituted an interim IRA, pending the enactment of comprehensive legislation.

It was on the basis of this report that the then Finance Minister P. Chidambaram proposed the opening up of insurance to the private sector, including multinational companies.

IRDA Bill

The IRDA Bill was drafted keeping the Malhotra Committee recommendations in view and hence the government has ruled out privatisation of public sector insurance companies, LIC and GIC. The bill did not provide for any dilution of 100 percent government equity in the two premier companies.

The IRDA bill sought to give a statutory status to the interim Insurance Regulatory Authority and amend the 1938 Insurance Act, the 1956 Life Insurance Corporation Act and the 1972 General Insurance Business (Nationalisation) Act to open up the sector. It provides for a nine-member regulatory body with statutory powers. The bill also fixed minimum capital requirement for life and general insurance at Rs.100 Crores and for reinsurance firms at Rs.200 Crores.

The Malhotra Committee Report justified the entry of foreign insurance companies by arguing that if it is permitted, it should be done on selective basis preferably through joint venture with Indian partner. In 1999, the bill was finally passed and IRDA was formed to regulate and promote insurance business in India.

The IRDA Act bestows the authority with powers to frame varies regulations, issue licenses, set capital requirements and solvency margins, prepare investment norms and inspect the books of private insurers independent of the government.

Liberalisation of Insurance Markets

Liberalisation of Insurance involves transformation of the industry from a Government monopoly to a competitive environment. Free markets allow for better resource allocation and creation of wealth and prosperity of people and the country. It enables development of health care, education and infrastructure of the country. In a liberalised insurance market, consumers are able to choose from different insurance providers having a wide range of products.

A liberal insurance market is one in which the market determines who should be allowed to sell insurance, what, how and the prices at which these insurance products should be sold. The issues like market access and equality of competitive opportunity and national treatment will decide who will be allowed to sell insurance. Second and fourth items commonly deal with issues such as product, price and market conduct regulation. There are certain pre-conditions to make liberalisation of insurance effective:

- Sound competition law
- Efficient and reliable regulation
- Phased liberalisation
- Consistency and impartiality between competitors
- Optimum quantum of regulation
- Efficient disclose and dissemination of information to the society.

Insurance markets in India possess certain imperfections justifying the need for competition as well as regulation.

INSURANCE PLAYERS IN INDIA

Bajaj Allianz General Insurance Company Limited

It is a joint venture between Bajaj Auto Limited and Allianz AG of Germany. The company registered on May 2, 2001 to conduct General Insurance business (including Health Insurance business) in India. The company has an authorised and paid up capital of Rs.110 Crores and has a network of 31 offices across the country.

ICICI Lombard General Insurance Company Limited

It is a joint venture between ICICI Bank Limited India's second largest bank and Lombard Canada Limited, one of the oldest property and casualty insurance companies in Canada. ICICI Lombard offers a wide range of retail and corporate general insurance customised products. The company has over 100 branches across the country.

IFFCO-TOKIO General Insurance Company Limited

It is a joint venture between IFFCO and The Tokio Marine and Fire Insurance Company Limited, Japan Krishak Bharati Cooperative Limited (KRIBHCO), and Indian Potash contributing 49 percent, 26 percent and 5 percent respectively to its Rs.100 Crores capital. After getting the licence the company started operations and is a leading private General Insurance Company in India in launching innovative insurance cover for farmers called the "Sankat Haran Policy" It is operating from 20 cities in India.

National Insurance Company Limited

It was incorporated in 1906 to carry out general insurance business and nationalised in 1972.In the same year, 22 foreign and 11 Indian Insurance Companies were amalgamated with National Insurance Company Limited, as a subsidiary company of General Insurance Corporation of India. In 2002, with the passage of Insurance amendment Bill (2002), National Insurance Company has been delinked from GIC and has been functioning as an independent company. Apart from domestic insurance business the company also undertakes reinsurance and foreign operations.

New India Assurance Company Limited

The New India Assurance Company was incorporated on July 23, 1919 and commenced business from October 14, 1919. In 1972 the Government of India took over the management of the company along with all other non-life insurers in the country. New India Assurance was subsequently reconstituted taking over 23 companies. In2002, with the passage of Insurance amendment Bill, New India Assurance Company Limited has been delinked from GIC and has been functioning as an independent company.

Oriental Insurance Company Limited

The Oriental Insurance Company Limited is a public sector company and is one of the four subsidiary companies of the General Insurance Corporation of India. In 1956, Oriental became a subsidiary of the Life Insurance Corporation of India.

On May 13, 1971 Government of India took over the management of all general insurance companies in India and nationalised the Oriental Fire and General Insurance Company under the General Insurance Corporation of India as one of the four subsidiaries. In 2002, with the passage of Insurance amendment Bill, the Oriental Insurance Company Limited has been delinked from GIC and has been functioning as an independent company.

United India Insurance Company Limited

United India Insurance is one of the four subsidiaries of the General Insurance Company carrying on general insurance business in India. In 2002, with the passage of Insurance amendment Bill (2002), United India Insurance has been delinked from GIC and has been functioning as an independent company.

Tata AIG General Insurance Company Limited

Tata AIG General Insurance Company Ltd. And Tata AIG Life Insurance Company Ltd. (collectively "Tata AIG") are joint venture companies between the Tata group and American International Group Inc. (AIG), the leading U.S. based international insurance and financial services organisation. It has a capital of Rs.125 Crores out of which 74 percent has been brought in by Tata Sons and the remaining 26 percent by American partner. Tata AIG General Insurance Company Limited claims to be the first Indian insurance company to offer a comprehensive policy to cover various risks in the IT sector.

Royal Sundaram General Insurance Company Limited

The joint venture between Royal and Sun Alliance Insurance and Sundaram Finance Limited started its operation from March 2001. Royal and Sun Alliance is one of the world's leading international insurance companies. The Sun was established in 1710 and is the oldest insurance company in existence still trading under its original name. The Alliance was founded in 1824 and the Royal in 1845.

Cholamandalam General Insurance Company Limited

It is promoted by Chennai based Murugappa Group. The company is founded with Rs.105 Crores out of which 75 percent is being held by Tube Investment, a Murugappa group company. While Cholamandalam Investment and Finance Company Limited holds 15 percent stake and the rest is by other privately held Murugappa companies with 5 percent stake each.

Reliance General Insurance Company Limited

Reliance group has announced its plans to enter the Indian insurance sector – both in the life and general insurance businesses. Reliance Industries plans to bring in around Rs.300 Crores into its insurance venture through its financial arm Reliance Capital Limited. The two companies will have an initial authorised capital of Rs.200 Crores each. This is the first Indian company without a foreign tie-up.

Export Credit Guarantee Corporation of India Limited

It was established in the year 1957 by the Government of India to strengthen the export promotion drive by covering the risk of exporting on credit. Being an export promotion organisation, it functions under the administrative control of the Ministry of Commerce, Government of India. It is the fifth largest credit insurer of the world in terms of coverage of national exports. The paid –up capital of the company is Rs.390 Crores.

HDFC Chubb General Insurance Limited

HDFC, India's premier financial services company and Chubb Corporation, leading global non-life insurer, entered into a joint venture agreement for non-life insurance in 2002. HDFC holds 74 percent and Chubb 26 percent in the joint venture company, HDFC Chubb General Insurance Limited with initial capital of Rs.100 Crores.

LIFE INSURERS

Alliance Bajaj Life Insurance Company Limited

Alliance Bajaj Life Insurance Company Limited is a joint venture between Alliance AG and Bajaj Auto Limited. The company was incorporated on March 12, 2001. The company received the IRDA certificate of registration on August 3, 2001 to conduct Life Insurance business in India.

Birla Sun Life Insurance Company Limited

It is a joint venture between Birla Group and Sun Life Corporation of U.S. The products of Birla Sun Life Insurance Company (BSLI) are distributed through a fully owned subsidiary– BSDL Insurance Advisory Services Limited (BSDL IAS) BSDL. The company claims to have unique products, presenting a powerful combination of returns, liquidity, safety, tax benefits, transparency and convenience.

HDFC Standard Life Insurance Company Limited

HDFC and Standard Life was the first joint venture to enter the life insurance market, in January 1995. In October 1998, the joint venture agreement was renewed and Standard Life purchased 2 percent of Infrastructure Development Finance Company Limited (IDFC).

The company as such, was incorporated on August 14, 2000 under the name of HDFC Standard Life Insurance Company Limited. HDFC are the main shareholders in HDFC Standard Life, with 81.4 percent, while Standard Life owns 18.6 percent. HDFC and Standard Life have a long and close relationship built upon shared values and trust.

ICICI Prudential Life Insurance Company Limited

The company was incorporated on July 20, 2000, with an authorised capital of Rs.230 Crores (paid up Rs.190 Crores). It is a joint venture of ICICI (74%) and Prudential plc U.K (26%). The company is on the top of the list of competitors to LIC. The company was granted certificate of incorporation on 26-11-2000 and it started its operations on 19-12-2000.

Life Insurance Corporation of India Limited

LIC was established in 1956 and is the dominant leader in life insurance in India. It has 7 zonal offices, over 100 divisional offices and 204 branches in India with over 6.50 lakhs agents.

Tata AIG Life Insurance Company Limited

It is capitalised at Rs.185 Crores of which 74 percent has been brought in by Tata Sons and the American partner brings in the remaining 26 percent. American Insurance Group (AIG) is the leading U.S. based international insurance and financial services organisation and the largest underwriter of commercial and industrial insurance in the United States. AIG's global businesses also include financial services and asset management. Including aircraft leasing, financial products, trading and market making, consumer finance, institutional, retail and direct investment fund asset management etc.

SBI Life Insurance Company Limited

India's largest bank SBI and Cardiff S.A. a leading insurer in France have firmed SBI Life. It is a 74: 24 venture; with Cardiff the foreign partner contributing 24 percent paid capital of Rs.250 Crores. SBI plans to market the insurance products through select branches of SBI and its seven associate banks.

OM Kotak Mahindra Insurance Company Limited

The joint venture OM Kotak Mahindra Life Insurance started off with an initial net worth of Rs.150 Crores, with 74: 26 stake between KMFL and OM. Kotak Mahindra is one of India's premier financial services groups, with a range of over two dozen highly specialised products and services. Starting as a one-product company in the mid 80's, they have evolved into a full service financial conglomerate. Old Mutual pic. Is a leading financial services provider in the world, providing a broad range of financial services in the area of insurance, asset management and banking. It is a leading life insurer in South Africa, with more than 30 percent market share. The partnership with Old Mutual plc. provides the Kotak Mahindra group with an international perspective and expertise in the life insurance business.

Max New York Life Insurance Company Limited

It is a partnership between Max India Limited, one of India's leading multi business corporations and New York Life, a Fortune 100 company. The paid up capital of the joint venture is Rs.250 Crores. Max India Ltd. is building businesses in the emerging knowledge based areas of Healthcare, Financial Services and Information Technology.

ING Vyasya Life Insurance Company Ltd.

It is a joint venture between ING, Vyasya Bank, one of India's leading private sector banks and GMR group. As per the joint venture agreement, Vyasya Bank holds 49 percent stake, ING 26 percent, and the GMR Group would hold 25 percent. The paid up capital of the joint venture is Rs.110 Crores. Vyasya Bank has a very high degree of retail focus with good customer service. ING Group, with an asset base of over Rs.28, 42,000 Crores is a global financial institution of Dutch origin, which is active in the field of banking, insurance and asset management in more than 60 countries.

Aviva Life Insurance Company Ltd.

It is a joint venture between Dabur India and CGU, a wholly owned subsidiary of Aviva Pic, is capitalised at Rs.110 Crores. Aviva Pic is the largest life and general insurance group of UK and the world's largest insurer with worldwide premium income and retail investment sales of £28 billion. Aviva Life has tied up with ABN Amro, Canara Bank, Laxmi Vilas Bank and American Express for distribution of its products.

AMP Sanmar Assurance Company Ltd.

It is a joint venture between AMP having a stake of 26 percent and the Sanmar Group holding 74 percent. The Sanmar group is one of the largest industrial groups in South India. AMP Limited is one of the world's leading financial services businesses.

6

ANNUAL REPORTS OF LIC AND GIC

The Annual Report of LIC

The contents of annual report of LIC are:

(1) Preamble Under Section 27 of the LIC Act 1956, LIC has to present its Annual report to the members. This also contains the names of the members of the Corporation and its various committees during the year.

(2) Scenario Economic In this, information is provided about GDP (Gross Domestic Product), GDS (Gross Domestic Saving), fiscal position, monetary conditions, inflation, equity market and external sector. What changes have taken place during the year in global life insurance business as well as domestic insurance market? After the opening up of the domestic insurance market in 1999 and with a level playing field provided by the new supervisory framework, what is the position of the state owned and private platers in the insurance business? How the changes in GDS, GDP and disposable income has affected the business performance of the insurance industry.

(3) Impact of Macro Economic Environment on Life Insurance Business Under this, the information is provided about impact of RBI policies and Government of India's Monetary and credit policies on insurance

business. Like there is a RBI policy to reduce the exposure of Non-Banking Financial Institutions including LIC, in the call money market. As a result the Corporation has reduced its investment in call money market to meet RBI guidelines. Now, LIC has been actively deploying its funds in other money market instruments like Repo and CBLO (Collateralized Borrowing and Lending Obligation). In addition, what is the impact of changes in the interest rate, inflation on life insurance business? Thus changes taking place on a global and national level affects the life insurance business.

(4) Working results the total working results of the Corporation are divided into two parts:

(1) New Business and

(2) Business in Force.

In new business the report discusses about the Number of Policies, Sum Assured, Annual Premium Receivable in Individual Assurance, General Annuity, Pensions Portfolio, Unit Linked business (Bema Plus and Future Plus) in India as well as out of India. It also gives information about Group insurance business including Social Security. In Social Security Schemes, the LIC provides insurance cover through Janashree Bima Yojana to 43 occupations like Beedi workers, Lady Tailors, Textile, Wood and Paper products, Printing, Physically Handicapped, Self-Employed persons.

The report also discusses about First Insurance, Rural Thrust, Alternate Distribution Channels, and Product Development. In First Insurance, in pursuance of the corporate objectives LIC provides insurance cover to more and more people who have no previous insurance on their lives. In Rural Thrust, LIC gives information about Life insurance cover provided to people of backward and remote areas. In Alternate Distribution

Channels, the LIC provides information about how in competitive market environment LIC targets new market segments and high net worth individuals to increase its customer base. Banks have emerged as strong business partners amongst alternate channels in terms of first premium mobilisation. In order to meet the changing needs of customers, LIC offers a wide variety of products. Thus, in product development, the LIC gives information about new insurance products introduced and some existing withdrawn from the market after periodical review of its product portfolio.

In Business In Force in various segments, the LIC report says about Number of Policies, Sum Assured, and Annual Premium Receivable under Individual Assurance, General Annuity Pension Portfolio, Unit Linked (Bima Plus and Future Plus) in India as well as out of India. In Group Insurance Business the information is given about Number of Schemes, Number of Members, Sum Assured, Premium Income under Group Insurance including Social Security and Group Superannuation.

(5) Capital Redemption and Annuity Certain Business it provides information about Annuity Certain and Capital Redemption Policies in force.

(6) Statutory Statements regarding Policies Under this heading information in statements in the form "DD" prescribed under Insurance Act, 1938 is given about Number of Policies, Sum Insured and Annuities Per Annum, Single Premiums and Yearly Renewal Premium for Ordinary policies (Individual Assurance), Annuity Contracts, Unit Linked Plans (Bima Plus and Future Plus), Jeevan Suraksha, Group Insurance Policies and Group Annuity Contracts etc. in India and out of India in respect of premium paid during the tear for New Life Insurance business. Statutory

Statements regarding Policies also provides information about Total Life Insurance business in force at the end of the year in the form of Number of Policies, Sum insured with Bonuses and Annuities per Annum, premium income for which credit has been taken in the Revenue Account in India and out of India.

(7) Life Fund, Surplus and Taxes Paid This provides information about life fund, valuation surplus, surplus retained, share of surplus and taxes paid to the Central Government for the last three years.

(8) Investments and Social Responsibilities This heading gives information about total investments of the Corporation in India and out of India. Besides investing in Stock Exchange Securities, Loans constitute one of the major avenues of investment for the Corporation's funds. Loans have been given to finance projects/ schemes for generation and transmission of electricity for agricultural and industrial use, housing schemes, development of road transport, piped water supply and sewerage projects in rural and urban areas and townships and industrial development.

LIC also fulfils its social responsibilities towards society at large.

To achieve this goal LIC provides security to as many people as possible. To meet this end, the Corporation has been promoting Social Welfare through socially oriented schemes. LIC invested and given loans to Central, State and other Government Guaranteed Marketable Securities and Infrastructure sector.

(9) Marketing Activities, Agents and Diversified Activities under marketing activities, LIC provides information about its operations in India and in Foreign countries.

Also its operations through Foreign Subsidiaries/ Joint Venture Companies. In Agents heading, LIC gives information about total number of agents on roll, number of schemes launched by the Corporation to promote the cause of professionalising the agency force. In order to recognize agents who perform consistently year after year, clubs at five levels have been designated viz. Chairman, Zonal Manager, Divisional Manager, Branch Manager and Distinguished Agents by the Corporation. In order to motivate and recognize high performers a premium club called the "Corporate Club" has been formed. Besides providing insurance covers to lakhs of people, how LIC has diversified its activities through LIC Housing Finance Limited, LIC Mutual Fund Trustee Company Private Limited/ Jeevan Bima Sahayog Asset Management Company (JBS AMC) Limited.

(10) Policy Holders' servicing this heading provides information about how Corporation settles the claims of policyholders on maturity as well as on death. In case Claimants have any grievances, they can present their cases before Zonal/ Central Claims Review Committee. To impart transparency to the decision making process former High Court / District Court Judge is appointed as a sitting member of Review Committee. Also Corporation has Grievance Redressal Officers at Branch / Divisional /Zonal / Central office to redress grievances of customers and for transparency.

(11) Public Relations and Corporate Communications Activities In order to improve public image and to boost the public confidence, Corporation has undergone a transformation, renaming its "PR and Publicity" department as "PR and CC" to revamp corporate image. AD campaigns through various media like Radio, TV, Internet, Press etc. were used to

augment its sales and to enhance brand image. For this LIC has received many accolades from diverse entities.

(12) Personnel and Employee Relations In this information is provided about staff strength, new recruitments, relationship with employees and unions, ratio of women workers in the total strength of staff, reservation of SC,ST and OBC, Physically Handicapped and Ex -- Servicemen Employees and Sports activities.

(13) HRD / OD initiatives / Training Statistics This heading provides information about training profiles of the Personnel of the Corporation. To sharpen the skills and capabilities of the personnel how training is imparted through in – house training centres, Management Development Centre, National Insurance Academy and Zonal and Divisional Training Centres. Besides this, to strengthen the entrepreneurial ability of the Managers to have better managerial perception and practices, Management Development Centre (MDC), the apex-training institute of LIC imparts training to Managers.

(14) Engineering Activities and Estates It gives information about new additions to the existing buildings and offices of the LIC. How Estate Portfolio of the Corporation progressed during the year, how much housing loans were given to employees for various staff housing schemes and agents housing schemes.

(15) Information Technology Initiatives This provides information about information technology initiatives undertaken by the Corporation to modernise their offices and to give better alternate options to the customers to do business with LIC like premium collection through ECS, E – Mail and Internet services,

on line Data Store Project, a standardised package for Pension Policy Servicing etc.

(16) Internal Audit To help management to take corrective action and to ensure continuous improvement in the overall working of the offices of the Corporation, internal audit department is established by the Corporation. It periodically audits the workings of Branch, Divisional and Zonal offices and all offices of the Corporation.

(17) Inspection and Vigilance Inspection of all the branches, Divisional and Zonal offices in India are carried out by the Corporation. Besides this, Vigilance activities are also undertaken by the Corporation. Here the greater emphasis is on preventive vigilance through the dissemination of information on areas susceptible to vigilance besides expediting disposal of vigilance cases.

(18) Nominee Directors It provides information of directors nominated by the Corporation on the Boards of the Companies where it has substantial stake by way of Debt or Equity. Nominee directors are reviewed and guided by the Corporation from time to time. These Directors are Non – Executive Directors, not connected with day to day operational matters of the Company, who report on important matters discussed at the board meetings/other related committee meetings or any other issue which deserves attention of the Corporation.

(19) Corporate Governance The practice of good Corporate Governance enables the strengthening of the confidence of the stake holders, maintaining a healthy industrial climate within the organisation improving customer focus and withstanding the pressures of change in the external environment and in making LIC is great and dynamic organisation. This is

achieved through various proactive measures, initiatives and guidance by the Government, namely, Board of Directors, Executive committee, Audit Committee, Investment Committee, Consumer Affairs Committee, Zonal Advisory Boards, Divisional level Policy holders Councils and LIC's employees and Agency force.

(20) Board Meetings and Central Management Committee As per regulations, Board meetings should be held at least once in a quarter. Board Meetings are generally held at corporate office of LIC to discuss policy matters to provide guidance and direction to management for Growth, Excellence and Corporate Governance. Board members have access to any information that they may like to have and the recommendations that may be prescribed or desired are implemented within the time frame. The Central Management Committee consists of all Executive Directors, Chief of Central Office and all the Zonal Managers. In the meetings Policy and Strategic issues are discussed and appropriate steps are taken to reformulate the strategies if thought necessary in view of the changes in the market environment.

(21) Zonal Advisory Board(ZAB) Zaps are constituted for each Zone, which are competent to discuss and review all matters and policy affecting the proper development of the LIC within due territorial limits of the Zone and make recommendations thereon.

(22) Policy Holder's Council Policyholder's councils are constituted in each division. Policyholder councils discuss all the matters, which relate to the servicing of the Policyholders. Items discussed are Service to the Policy Holder, Outstanding claims, Progress of New Business in the Division, Publicity activities etc.

(23) Auditors Appointment of Statutory Auditors with the previous approval of the Central Government. In this

the names and addresses of the firms are given.

(24) Plans In this, information about Annual Budget of New Business is given. This heading provides for what LIC wishes to do in the coming financial year under:

(1) Linked Business
- Life Assurance
- Pension Plan
- Total linked Business

(2) Non-linked Business
- Life Assurance
- Pension plan
- Total Linked Business

(3) Composite Business

(25) Acknowledgement In this LIC expresses its sincere thanks to the various Parliamentary Committees, the Union Finance Minister, and Union Minister of state for Finance, the Insurance division of the ministry of Finance and the IRDA for their active support, advice and cooperation on various committees and Board of Directors for their guidance and valuable suggestions.

The Annual Report of GIC

The Annual Report of a GIC has the following contents:

(1) Information about Corporation, board of Directors and Management It provides information about the members of the board of directors, Auditors bankers and registered office of the GIC. It also gives information about composition of the Management, like the names of Chairman-cum-Managing Director, Chief Vigilance officer and Assistant General Manager

(2) Notices It incorporates information about notice given to all the members about Annual General meeting to

transact the business. This notice provides information about when and where the meeting will be held and what will be discussed in the meeting. The notice gives opportunity to the members who are unable to attend the meeting on the designated place that they can appoint another person as his/her proxy to attend the meeting and thereat instead of him/her.

(3) Director's report In this, the director represents the annual report on the working and affairs of the Corporation and the audited statement of account for the year ended to the members. This is the important document as it provides information about financial results of the corporation for the year under review. It informs about the total authorised and paid-up of the corporation, whether any new issues or bonus shares have been issued during the year, what rate of dividend has been proposed by directors. What is the position of capital and funds, assets, investments of the corporation in the current year? Whether there is any increase or decrease as compared to the previous year. As GIC is a Reassurance Company, its working and functions, are governed by the IRDA. So it has to confirm to the requirements of the IRDA about paid-up equity specifications, preparations and presentation of financial statements and auditor's report.

The director's report also provides information about total strength of the corporation, total amount of remuneration paid to the employees, welfare schemes undertaken, if any, for the welfare of the employees like SC/ST?OBC etc., to upgrade the skills of the officers and staff,any training programmes undertaken by the corporation.

The report discloses the names of the board of directors, different board committees like audit committee and investment committee and their composition. To ensure financial and office discipline and also to imbibe a culture of value and ethics in daily office work, vigilance department is constituted which is headed by a chief vigilance officer. There is also an internal audit department in the corporation. The directors present information about how internal audit department conducts audit of business transactions and also renews prevalent systems and makes suggestions and recommendations for the consideration of the Audit committee of the board. And lastly they give information about the domestic as well as the overseas operation of the corporation, their responsibilities to confirm to the requirements of sec217 (2AA) of the companies Act 1956, about observation of applicable accounting standards in the preparation of annual accounts, consistent application of accounting policies and about precautions and care taken to safeguard the assets of the corporation and for prevention and detection of frauds and other irregularities.

(4) Management's discussion and Analysis Report In this management discusses about global economic scenario, in particular Indian economic conditions and the factors which effect the economic conditions. All these factors contribute towards the growth of insurance industry on a global scale and affect Indian insurance industry also.

It also discusses business performance in terms of total premium earned from different classes of business, income from investments, apportionment of overall revenue profit among the policyholders' fund and payment of claims to policyholders'.

It also provides information about global risks affecting the insurance business like Terrorism, Natural Perils,

Liability, Environmental issues etc. In order to mitigate these risks, management exchanges information about all these risks with various global players in the insurance market. Besides Global risks, Strategic risks also affect the functioning of the Corporation. Strategic risks arise from an imbalance between the defined corporate strategy and the constantly fluctuating business environment. To reduce such risks, monitoring of mission – critical parameters and regular review of underlying assumptions are done by the management.

As GIC is reinsurance company, Operational risks (technical) is of special importance to it. The risk factors that can affect business are appropriate pricing, accurate estimates of claims liability and establishing adequate reserves for catastrophic losses. To reduce such risks GIC adopts a very conservative loss reserving methodology.

An operational risk (investment) is another type of operational risks. Investment risks mainly consist of market fluctuations, quality of the investments (security ratings) and liquidity. GIC's debt portfolio being of high quality enjoys liquidity benefits and least of credit risk. Corporation follows an active investment policy to earn better returns. Future outlook of GIC provides information about its future plans. What actions will be taken by the Corporation to achieve these objectives? How it will sense the opportunities to strengthen its position in the domestic as well as international markets to face new threats and challenges.

(5) Management Report In this, in accordance with Part IV of schedule B of the IRDA (Preparation of Financial Statements and Auditor's Report of Insurance Companies) Regulations 2002, the management of the Corporation confirms that all dues payable to the

statutory authorities have been duly paid, shareholding pattern as well as transfer of shares is in accordance with the regulatory or statutory requirements, required solvency margins have been maintained and that the Corporation's risk exposure consists of Obligatory Cessions, Facultative Support given to Indian Insurance Companies, Corporation's share in Indian Insurance Companies through First/ Second Surplus Treaties and Excess of Loss programme and also Foreign Inward Business accepted.Besides this Corporation also declares and certifies that funds of the holders of policies in India are not directly or indirectly invested outside India, the values of all the assets of the Corporation have been reviewed on the date of the Balance Sheet, that the Corporation does not operate directly in any other country except through its representative offices. The Corporation also confirms that applicable accounting standards, principles and policies have been followed consistently in the preparation of financial statements and sufficient care has been taken for safeguarding the assets of the company as well for prevention and detection of fraud and other irregularities and in the last financial statements are prepared on a going concern basis and internal audit system commensurate with the size and nature of the business exists and is operating effectively. The management also certifies that no payment has been made to individuals, firms, companies and organisations in which the Directors of the corporation are interested.

(6) Comments and Review by Comptroller and Auditor General of India under sec. 619(4) of the Companies Act, 1956 on the accounts of GIC.

(7) Auditors' report In this auditors appointed by the Corporation, audit the attached Balance Sheet of GIC and also the Revenue Accounts of Fire, Marine,

Miscellaneous and Life reinsurance and the Profit and Loss Account and the Cash Flow Statement for the year ended on that date annexed thereto. In this report the auditors express their opinion on these financial statements and report to the members of the Corporation that proper books of account have been maintained and the Balance Sheet, Revenue Accounts and Profit and Loss Account and Cash Flow Statement comply with the Accounting Standards as well as IRDA regulations. Auditors also have to certify that after reviewing the management report no apparent mistake or material inconsistencies have been found.

(8) Schedules forming part of Financial Statements In the schedules information about premium earned (net), claims incurred (net) on different forms of insurance, commission paid, about Share Capital, Share Capital pattern of Shareholding, Reserves and Surplus, Investments – Shareholders' fund and Policyholders' Fund, Loans, Fixed Assets, Cash and Bank Balances, Advances and Other Assets, Current Liabilities, Provisions and Miscellaneous Expenditure is given.

In the end we can sum up that Insurance is a financial arrangement for redistributing the costs of unexpected losses requiring a legal contract whereby an insurer agrees to compensate an insured for loss. A loss is an undesired, unplanned reduction of economic value. The benefits of insurance are too large that it is beneficial for individual as well as business organisations to insure their properties and themselves against uncalled for contingencies.

The principles of Insurance provide us information about those features on which the whole insurance business is based. Types of insurance as well as new insurance products provide us information about availability of different types of insurance covers in the market and different policies under all these categories. It also gives information about new products offered by new players in the market after the opening up of the insurance industry to foreign and multinational companies. What changes that have made in the Indian Insurance Industry. In the next lesson you will study the different Acts and Laws, which has changed the face of the insurance industry in India especially the IRDA Act.

LEGAL FRAMEWORK

Insurance is a tool used to help manage financial risk. Financial risk can take many forms. There are risks to our investments, liabilities for our actions, and risks to our ability to earn income. There is insurance to manage all these risks. Insurance is a financial agreement entered by two people to protect one against a certain risk. The contract that binds the two parties to certain obligations is known as Policy. The one who buys the insurance is known as policyholder or insured while the party that sells insurance is known as the insurer. From the time the insured signs the policy he/she has an obligation to pay a certain amount of money known as premium.. In this lesson, we will discuss the various laws governing insurance in India. The Insurance sector in India is governed by Insurance Act, 1938, the Life Insurance Corporation Act, 1956 and General Insurance Business (Nationalization) Act, 1972, Insurance Regulatory and Development Authority (IRDA) Act, 1999 and other related acts.

Objectives

After going through this lesson you should be able to:

- Define the term contract.
- Describe essential features of valid contract.
- Understand meaning of lawful Consideration.
- Define the term 'Consumer'.

- Know the difference between agent and servant.
- Define Complaint Procedure.
- Know redressal of consumer's grievances
- Understand Features of IRDA Act.
- Understand main functions of LIC Act.
- Understand main functions of GIC Act

GENERAL CONTRACT ACT 1872, LIC ACT 1956 & GIC ACT 1972

Essentials of General Contract (Section 10) of Indian Contract Act 1872

A contract is an agreement made between two or more parties, which the law will enforce. To be enforceable by law, an agreement must possess the essential elements of a valid contract as contained in Sections 10.

Essential of a valid contract: The contract of insurance, like any other contract must fulfill the following essential requirements of a valid contract as laid down in the Indian contracts act.

A contract is an agreement made between two or more parties, which the law will enforce.

The essential requirements of a valid contract as laid down in the Indian contract act are:

1. *Agreement*: This involves, one party making the offer and the other party accepting it. The acceptance of the offer must be in the writing or given verbally and must be absolute and unconditional and must be communicated to the proposer.
2. *Legal Relationship*: when the two parties enter into an agreement their intention must be create legal relationship between them. With many informal and social agreements, such as, an agreement to give a

friend a lift in one's car, there is never any intention of legal consequences so the agreement for same reason should not be carried out

3. *Lawful Consideration*: The, agreement is legally enforceable, only when the contract is supported by consideration, i.e., 'when both the parties give something in return. In insurance both parties provide consideration. Consideration from the insured to the insurer is the premium while from the insurer to the insured is a promise to compensate the insured or to make certain payment in the event of certain happening s taking place.
4. *Capacity of Parties*: The parties to the agreement must be competent or capable of entering into a valid contract. A person is competent to contract if he is of the age of majority, is sound mind, and is not disqualified from contracting by any law to which he is subject
5. *Free and Genuine Consent*: There must also be a free and genuine consent of the parties to the agreement. If the agreement is induced by 44 coercion, undue influence, fraud misrepresentation etc., there is absence of free consent.
6. *Lawful Object*: The object of the contract must be lawful. Thus, the object of the agreement must not be illegal, immoral, or opposed to public policy. If an agreement suffers from any legal flaw, it would not be enforceable by law. For example a landlord knowingly lets a house to terrorist to carry out his activities, and he cannot recover the rent through the court of law.
7. *Agreement Not Declared Void*: The agreement, though it might possess all the essential elements, must not have been expressly declared void by any law in force in country. Any contract which is contrary to the

law of this country is void, such as insurance on goods being traded with an enemy national in times of war.

8. *Certainty and Possibility or Performance*: It is essential the creation of every contract that the terms of agreement must be certain and not vague, indefinite, or ambiguous. An agreement to do an act impossible in itself cannot be enforced. For example Q agrees with P, to increase his height by magic. This agreement is not enforceable by law.

9. *Legal Formalities*: The agreement maybe either oral or in writing. But if it is in writing, it must comply with the necessary legal formalities as to writing, registration, attestation, and stamp and must be issued under seal.

CONTRACTS WHICH ARE DEFECTIVE

Void Agreement: An agreement not enforceable by law is said to be void [sec2 (g)]. A void agreement does not create any legal rights or obligations. It is void ab initio, i.e. from very beginning, for example an agreement with minor. Void contracts: A contracts which legally does not exist is known as void contract. In other words, a contract, which ceases to be enforceable, is void when it ceases to be enforceable. It is valid when it is entered into, but something, which happens subsequently to the formation of the contract makes it void. Example: a contract to import goods from foreign country. It may subsequently become void.

Voidable Contract: An agreement which is enforceable by law at the option of one or more of the parties thereto, but not at the option of the other or others, is voidable contract. In other words when either party is in breach of the essential terms of the contract, the other party has a right to consider the contract void. If the aggrieved party may decide to overlook the breach or to waive the breach, the contract on this case is unaffected and remains in full force. Example: Anu promises to sell his watch for Rs. 500. Her consent is obtained by use of force. The contract is voidable at the option of Anu. She may accept it or reject it. Unenforceable contracts: Unenforceable contracts are those which are neither void nor voidable but which cannot be enforced through the courts. For example, an insurance policy without proper stamp duty cannot be produced as evidence of a contract in court. Unenforceable contracts are fully valid contracts but the parties cannot enforce them through the courts.

Illegal Agreements: Illegal agreements are those agreements, which involve the breaking of some rule of basic public policy and.are criminal in nature. An illegal agreement is not only void as between immediate parties but also taints the collateral transactions with illegality.

Essential Feature of Insurance Contracts

The purchasers of Insurance have to enter into a contract, where by one party (insured) agrees to pay to other party (insurer) a certain sum of money, determined on the happening of a certain event in consideration of a certain sum of money caned Premium. Such a contract is known as "Insurance Contract". Like any other contract, Insurance contract are also governed by the provisions of the law of contract as laid down in The Indian Contract Act, 1872. Therefore they have to fulfill the essential features of a valid contract. The essentials of a valid contract have been discussed earlier.

Life Insurance Corporation Act, 1956

An Act to provide for the nationalization of life insurance business in India by transferring all such business to a Corporation established for the purpose and to provide for the regulation and control of the business of the Corporation and for matters connected there with or incidental thereto.

Some of the important provisions are as follows: —

1. Short title and commencement. —

(1) This Act maybe called the Life Insurance Corporation Act, 1956

(2) It shall come into force on such date as the Central Government may, by Notifications in the Official Gazette, appoint. Definitions: In this Act, unless the context otherwise requires,

(1) "Appointed day," means the date on which the Corporation is established under Section 3;

(2) "Composite insurer "means an insurer carrying on in addition to controlled business any other kind of insurance business;

(3) "Controlled business" means—

(i) In the case of any insurer specified in sub-clause (a) or sub-clause (b) of clause (9) of section 2 of the Insurance Act and carrying on life insurance business—

(a) all his business, if he carries on no other class of insurance business;

(b) all the business appertaining to his life insurance business, if he carries on any other class of insurance business also;

(c) all his business if his certificate of registration under the Insurance Act in respect of general insurance business stands wholly cancelled for a period of more than six months on the 19th day of January, 1956.

(ii) in the case of any other insurer specified in clause (9) ofsection2 of the Insurance Act and carrying on life insurance business—

(a) all his business in India, if he carries on no other class of insurance business in India;

(b) all the business appertaining to his life insurance business in India, if he carries on any other class of insurance business also in India;

(c) all his business in India if he certificate of registration under the Insurance Act in respect of general insurance business in India stands wholly cancelled for a period of more than six months on the 19th day of January, 1956.

Explanation

An insurer is said to carry on no class of insurance business other than life insurance business,if in addition to life insurance business, he carries on only capital redemption business or annuity certain business or both;and the expression" business appertaining to his life insurance business" in sub-clause (i) and (ii) shall be construed accordingly; (iii) in the case of a provident society, as defined in section 65 of the Insurance; Act, all its business; (iv) in the case of the Central Government or a State Government, all life insurance business carried on by it, subject to the exceptions specified in section44;

(4) "Corporation" means the Life Insurance Corporation of India established under section 3;

(5) "Insurance Act" means the Insurance Act, 1938(4of1938);

(6) "Insurer" means an insurer as defined in the Insurance Act who carries on life insurance business in India and includes the Government and a provident society as defined in section65 of the Insurance Act;

(7) "Member" means a member of the Corporation;

(8) "Prescribed" means prescribed by rules made under this Act;

(9) "Tribunal" means a Tribunal constituted under section17 and having jurisdiction in respect of any matter under the rules made under this Act;

(10) All other words and expressions used herein but not defined and defined in the Insurance Act shall have the meanings respectively assigned to them in that Act.

Establishment and incorporation of Life Insurance Corporation of India.—

(1) With effect from such date as the Central Government may, by notification in the Official Gazette, appoint, there shall be established a Corporation called the Life Insurance Corporation of India.

(2) The Corporation shall be a body corporate having perpetual succession and a common seal with power subject to the provisions of this Act, to acquire, hold and dispose of property, and may by its name sue and be sued.

Constitution of the Corporation

(1) The Corporation shall consist of such number of persons not exceeding 2 as the Central Government may think fit to appoint thereto and one of them shall be appointed by the Central Government to be the Chairman there of.

(2) Before appointing a person to be a member, the Central Government shall satisfy itself that person will have no such financial or other interest as is likely to affect prejudicially the exercise or performance by him of his functions as a member, and the Central Government shall also satisfy itself from time to time with respect to every member that he has no such interest; and any person who is, or whom the Central

Government proposes to appoint and who has consented to be, a member shall, whenever required by the Central Government so to do, furnish to it such information as the Central Government considers necessary for the performance of its duties under this sub-section.

(3) A member who is in anyway directly or indirectly interested in a contract made or proposed to be made by the Corporation shall as soon as possible after the relevant circumstances have come to his knowledge, disclose the nature of his interest to the Corporation and the member shall not take part in any deliberation or discussion of the Corporation with respect to that contact.

Capital of the Corporation.—

(1) The original capital of the Corporation shall be five crores of rupees provided by the Central Government after due appropriation made by Parliament bylaw for the purpose, and the terms and conditions relating to the provision of such capital shall be such as maybe determined by the Central Government.

(2) The Central Government may, on the recommendation of the Corporation, reduce the capital of the Corporation to such extent and in such manner as the Central Government may determine.

Functions of the Corporation

1) Subject, to the rules, if any, made by the Central Government in this behalf, it shall be the general duty of the Corporation to carry on life insurance business, whether in or outside India, and the Corporation shall so exercise its powers under this Act as to secure that life insurance business is developed to the best advantage of the community.

2) Without prejudice to the generality of the provisions contained in sub-section (1) but subject to the other provisions contained in this Act, the Corporation shall have power —

(a) To carryon capital redemption business, annuity certain business or reinsurance business in so far as such re insurance business appertains to life insurance business;

(b) Subject to the rules, if any, made by the Central Government in this behalf, to invest the funds of the Corporation in such manner as the Corporation may think fit and to take all such steps as may be necessary or expedient for the protection or realization of any investment; including the taking over of and administering any property offered as security for the investment until a suitable opportunity arises for its disposal;

(c) To acquire, hold and dispose of any property for the purpose of its business;

(d) To transfer the whole or any part of the life insurance business carried on outside India to any other person or persons, if in the interest of the Corporation it is expedient so to do;

(e) To advance or lend money upon the security of any movable property or otherwise;

(f) To borrow or raise any money in such manner and upon such security as the Corporation may think fit;

(g) To carry on either by itself or through any subsidiary any other business in any case where such other business was being carried on by a subsidiary of an insurer whose controlled business has been transferred to and invested in the Corporation under this Act;

(h) to carry on any other business which may seen to the Corporation to be capable of being conveniently carried on in connection with its business and calculated directly or indirectly to render profitable the business of the corporation;

(i) to do all such things as maybe incidental or conducive to the proper exercise of any of the powers of the Corporation. In the discharge of any of its functions the Corporation shall act so far as maybe on business principles.

Power to Impose Conditions, etc.

(1) In entering into any arrangement, under section 6, with any concern, the Corporation may impose such conditions as it may think necessary or expedient for protecting the interest of the Corporation and for securing that the accommodation granted by it is put to the best use by the concern.

(2) Where any arrangement entered into by the Corporation under section 6 with any concern provides for the appointment by the Corporation of one or more directors of such concern, such provision and any appointment of directors made in pursuance there of shall be valid and effective notwithstanding anything to the contrary contained in the Companies Act, 1956 (1 of1956),or in any other law for the time being in force or in the memorandum, articles of association or any other instrument relating to the concern, and any provision regarding share, qualification, age limit, number of directorships, removal from office of Directors and such like conditions contained in any such law or instrument aforesaid, shall not apply to any director appointed by the Corporation in pursuance of the arrangement as aforesaid.

(3) Any director appointed as aforesaid shall-

(a) Hold office during the pleasure o f the Corporation any maybe removed or substituted by any person by order in writing by the Corporation;

(b) Not incur any obligation or liability by reason only of his being a director or for anything done or omitted to be done in good faith in the discharge of his duties as a director or anything in relation thereto;

(c) Not be liable to retirement by rotation and shall not be taken into account for computing the number of directors liable to such retirement.

Offices, Branches and Agencies

(1) The central office of the Corporation shall be at such place as the Central Government may, by notification in he Official Gazette, specify.

(2) The Corporation shall establish a zonal office at each of the following places, namely, Bombay, Calcutta, Delhi, Kanpur and Madras, and, subject to the previous approval of the Central Government, may establish such other zonal offices as it thinks fit.

(3) The territorial limits of each zone shall be such as may be specified by the Corporation.

(4) There may be established as many divisional offices and branches in each zone as the Zonal Manager thinks fit.

Committees of the Corporation

(1) The Corporation may entrust the general superintendence and direction of its affairs and business to an Executive Committee consisting of not more than five of its members and the Executive

Committee may exercise all powers and do all such acts and things as may be delegated to it by the Corporation.

(2) The Corporation may also constitute an Investment Committee for the purpose of advising it in matters relating to the investment of its funds, and the Investment Committee shall consist of not more than eight members of whom not less than four shall be members of the Corporation and the remaining members shall be persons (whether members of the Corporation or not) who have special knowledge and experience in financial matters, particularly, matters relating to investment of funds.

(3) The Corporation may constitute such other Committees as it may thin fit for the purpose of discharging such of its functions as maybe delegated to them.

Funds of the Corporation

The Corporation shall have its own fund and all receipts of the Corporation shall be credited thereto and all payments of the Corporation shall be made there from. Audit.—

(1) The accounts of the Corporation shall be audited by auditors duly qualified to act as auditors of companies under the law for the time being in force relating to companies, and the auditors shall be appointed by the Corporation with the previous approval of the Central Government and shall receive such remuneration from the Corporation as the Central Government may fix.

(2) Every auditor in the performance of his duties shall have at all reasonable times access to the books, accounts and other documents of the Corporation.

(3) The auditors shall submit their report to the Corporation and shall also forward a copy of their report to the Central Government.

ANNUAL REPORT OF ACTIVITIES OF CORPORATION

The Corporation shall, as soon as may be, after the end of each financial year, prepare and submit to the Central Government in such form as maybe prescribed a report giving an account of its activities during the previous financial year, and the report shall also give an account of the activities, if any, which are likely to be undertaken by the Corporation in the next financial year.

General Insurance Contract, 1972

Although Life Insurance was nationalized as early as 1956, general insurance business continued to be in the private sector right up to 1969. In that year the Government imposed strict social control on General Insurance Companies. This was a prelude to nationalization of General of General Insurance Business. With effect from 13th May, 1971 under the provisions of General Insurance (Emergency Provisions) Act, 1971 the Government of India took over the management of all General Insurance Companies operating in India whether they belonged to Indian or non-Indian shareholders.

Subsequently, the General Insurance (Emergency Provisions) Amendment Act, 1971 was passed withdrawing certain rights of the Directors and Members of the Companies, which they were enjoying under the Companies Act. General Insurance (Nationalization) Act, 1972 shortly followed and with effect from 2nf January, 1973 the provisions of the Act became effective. The functions of the Corporation are enumerated in Section18 of the Act, some of are as follows:

Functions of Corporation –

(1) The functions of the Corporation shall include:-

(a) The carrying on of any part of the general insurance business, if it thinks it desirable to do so;

(b) Aiding, assisting and advising the acquiring companies in the matter of setting up of standards of conduct and sound practice in general insurance business and in the matter of rendering efficient services to holders of policies of general insurance;

(c) Advising the acquiring companies in the matter of the controlling their expenses including the payment of commission and other expenses.

(d) Advising the acquiring companies in the matter of the investment of their funds;

(e) Issuing directions to acquiring companies in relation to the conduct of general insurance business.

(2) In issuing any directions under sub-section (1), the Cooperation shall keep in mind the desirability of encouraging composition amongst the acquiring companies as far as possible in order to render their services more efficient."

Functions of acquiring companies:-

(1) Subject to the rules, if any, made by the Central Government in this behalf and to its memorandum and articles of association, it shall be the duty of every acquiring company to carry on general insurance business.

(2) Each acquiring company shall so function under this Act as to secure that general insurance business is developed to the best of the community.

(3) In the discharge of any of its functions, each acquiring company shall act so far as may be on business principles and where any directions have been issued by the Corporation shall be guided by such directions.

(4) For the removal of doubts it is hereby declared that the Corporations and any acquiring company may,

subject to the rules, if any, made by the Central Government in this behalf, "enter into such contracts of reinsurance treaties as it may think fit for the protection of its interests".

Under Sec. 35, The Central Government may by notification specify the application of the provision of the Insurance Act with such modifications as is deemed necessary to the Corporation and the acquiring companies. The Central Government is also empowered to make rules to carry out the provisions of the Act and such rules may provide for:

(a) Manner in which the profits and other moneys received by the Corporation may be dealt with'

(b) The conditions subject to which the Corporation and the acquiring companies shall carry on general insurance business;

(c) The terms and conditions subject to which any re-insurance contract or treaties may be entered into;

(d) Form and manner in which any notice or application may be made to the Central Government;

(e) The reports which may be called for by the Central Government from the Corporation and acquiring companies; and

(f) Any other matter which is required to be or may be prescribed.

THE INSURANCE ACT, 1938

Earlier to the Insurance Act, 1938, the insurance business was carried by the insurance companies in accordance with the principles of the Company Law, 1913. When the business started growing, the need for an independent law to regulate the insurance business was noticed and a separate Act, the Insurance Act, 1938 was legislated.

The Act was used for all purposes relating to both life and general insurance businesses and their regulations. With regards to general insurance, this Act is being used to regulate the marine insurance, fire insurance and other insurances. Further growth of business has made it complex and more legal provisions were required to regulate it. The Marine Insurance Act, 1963, Public Liability Insurance Act, 1991, Insurance Regulatory and Development Authority Act, 1999 and regulations made by the IRDA are some of the legislations that govern the insurance business.

Short Title, Extent and Commencement

1. (1) This Act may be called Insurance Act, 1938.

(2) It extends to the whole of India.

(3) It shall come into force on such date3 as the Central Government may, by Notification in the Official Gazette, appoint in this behalf.

Definitions.

2. In this Act, unless there is anything repugnant in the subject or context,-

(1) "Authority" means the Insurance Regulatory and Development Authority established under sub-section (1) of section 3 of the Insurance Regulatory and Development Authority Act, 1999;

(2) "Policy-holder" includes a person to whom the whole of the interest of the policy-holder in the policy is assigned once and for all, but does not include an assignee thereof whose interest in the policy is infeasible or is for the time being subject to any condition;

(3) "Approved securities," means-

(i) Government securities and other securities charged on the revenue of the Central Government or of the Government of a State or guaranteed fully as regards principal and interest by the Central Government or the Government of any State;

(ii) debentures or other securities for money issued under the authority of any Central Act or Act of a State Legislature by or on behalf of a port trust or municipal corporation or city improvement trust in any Presidency-town;

(iii) shares of a corporation established by law and guaranteed fully by the Central Government or the Government of a State as to the repayment of the principal and the payment of the divided;

(iv) securities issued or guaranteed fully as regards principal and interest by the Government of any Part B State and specified as approved securities for the purposes of this Act by the Central Government by notification in the Official Gazette; and

(4) "Auditor" means a person qualified under the Chartered Accountants Act, 1949 (38 of 1949), to act as an auditor of companies;

(4A) "Banking company" and "company" shall have the meanings respectively assigned in them in clauses (c) and (d) of sub-section (1) of Section 5 of the Banking Companies Act, 1949 (10 of 1949);

(5) "Certified" in relation to any copy or translation of a document required to be furnished by or on behalf of an insurer or a provident society as defined in Part III means certified by a principal officer of 6Esuch insurer or provident society to be a true copy or a correct translation, as the case may be;

(5A) "Chief agent" means a person who, not being a salaried employee of an insurer, in consideration of any commission-

(i) Performs any administrative and organizing functions for the insurer, and

(ii) Procures life insurance business for the insurer by employing or causing to be employed insurance agents on behalf of the insurer;

(5-B) "Controller of Insurance" means the officer appointed by the Central Government under section 2B to exercise all the powers, discharge the functions and performs the duties of the Authority under this Act or the Life Insurance Corporation Act, 1956 (31 of 1956) or the General Insurance Business (Nationalization) Act, 1972 (57 of 1972) or the Insurance Regulatory and Development Authority Act, 1999;]

(6) "Court" means the principal Civil Court of original jurisdiction in a district and includes the High Court in exercise of its ordinary original civil jurisdiction;

(6A) "Fire insurance business" means the business of effecting, otherwise than incidentally to some other class of insurance business, contracts of insurance against loss by or incidental to fire or other occurrence customarily included among the risks insured against in fire insurance Policies;

(6B) "General insurance business" means fire, marine or miscellaneous insurance business, whether carried on singly or in combination with one or more of them;

(7) "Government security" means a Government security as defined in the Public Debt Act, 1944 (18 of 1944);

(7A) "Indian insurance company" means any insurer being a company-

(a) which is formed and registered under the Companies Act, 1956 (1 of 1956);

(b) in which the aggregate holdings of equity shares by a foreign company, either by itself or through its subsidiary companies or its nominees, do not exceed twenty-six percent paid-up equity capital of such Indian insurance company;

(c) whose sole purpose is to carry on life insurance business or general insurance business or re-insurance business.

(8) "Insurance company" means any insurer being a company, association or partnership which may be wound up under the Indian Companies Act, 1913 (7 of 1913), or to which the Indian Partnership Act, 1932 (9 of 1932), applies;

(9) "Insurer" means-

(a) any individual or unincorporated body of individuals or body corporate incorporated under the law of any country other than India, carrying on insurance business not being a person specified in sub-clause (c) of this clause which-

(i) carries on that business in India, or

(ii) has his or its principal place of business or is domiciled in India, or

(iii) with the object of obtaining insurance business, employs a representative, or maintains a place of business, in India;

(b) any body corporate [not being a person specified in sub-clause (c) of this clause] carrying on the business of insurance, which is a body corporate incorporated under any law for the time being in force in India; or stands to any such body corporate in the relation of a subsidiary company within the meaning of the Indian Companies Act, 1913 (7 of 1913), as defined by sub-section (2) of section 2 of that Act, and

(c) any person who in India has a standing contract with underwriters who are members of the Society

of Lloyd's whereby such person is authorized within the terms of such contract to issue protection notes, cover notes, or other documents granting insurance cover to others on behalf of the underwriters. But does not include a principal agent' chief agent, special agent' or an insurance agent or a provident society as defined in Part III;

(10) "Insurance agent" means an insurance agent licensed under Sec. 42 who receives agrees to receive payment by way of commission or other remuneration in consideration of his soliciting or procuring insurance business including business relating to the continuance, renewal or revival of policies of insurance;

(10A) "investment company" means a company whose principal business is the acquisition of shares, stocks debentures or other securities;

(10B) "Intermediary or insurance intermediary" shall have the meaning assigned to it in clause (f) of sub-section 2 of the Insurance Regulatory and Development Authority Act, 1999 (41 of 1999)

(11) "Life insurance business" means the business of effecting contracts of insurance upon human life, including any contract whereby the payment of money is assured on death (except death by accident only) or the happening of any

(12) "Manager" and "officer" have the meanings assigned to those expressions in clauses (9) and (11), respectively of Section 2 of the Indian Companies Act, 1913 (7 of 1913);

(13) " Managing agent" means a person, firm or company entitled to the management of the whole affairs of a company by virtue of an agreement with the company, and under the control and direction of the directors except to the extent, if any, otherwise provided for in the agreement, and includes any person, firm or

company occupying such position by whatever name called.

Explanation. —If a person occupying the position of managing agent calls himself manager or managing director, he shall nevertheless be regarded as managing agent for the purposes of Sec. 32 of this Act;

(13A) "marine insurance business" means the business of effecting contracts of insurance upon vessels of any description, including cargoes, freights and other interests which may be legally insured, in or in relation to such vessels, cargoes and freights, goods, wares, merchandise and property of whatever description insured for any transit, by land or water, or both, and whether or not including warehouse risks or similar risks in addition or as incidental to such transit, and includes any other risks customarily included among the risks insured against in marine insurance policies;

(13B) "miscellaneous insurance business" means the business of effecting contracts of insurance which is not principally or wholly of any kind or kinds included in clause (6A), (11) and (13A);

(14) "Prescribed" means prescribed by rules made under this Act; and

(15) "Principal agent" means a person who, not being a salaried employee of an insurer, in consideration of any commission,—

(i) Performs any administrative and organizing functions for the insurer; and

(ii) Procures general insurance business whether wholly or in part by employing or causing to be employed insurance agents on behalf of the

(16) "Private company" and "public company" have the meanings respectively assigned to them in Clauses

(13) and (13-A) of Sec. 2 of the Indian Companies Act, 1913 (7 of 1913);

(17) "Special agent" means a person who, not being a salaried employee of an insurer, in consideration of any commission, procures life insurance business for the insurer whether wholly or in part by employing or causing to be employed insurance agents on behalf of the insurer, but does not include a chief agent.

Appointment of Authority of Insurance

(1) If at any time, the Authority is superseded under sub-section (1) of section19 of the Insurance Regulatory and Development Authority Act, 1999, the Central Government may, by notification in the Official Gazette, appoint a person to be the Controller of Insurance till such time the Authority is reconstituted under subsection (3) of section 19 of that Act.

(2) In making any appointment under this section, the Central Government shall have due regard to the following considerations, namely, whether the person to be appointed has had experience in industrial, commercial or insurance matter and whether such person has actuarial qualifications. Requirements as to capital.

No insurer carrying on the business of life insurance, general insurance or re58 insurance in India on or after the commencement of the Insurance Regulatory and Development authority Act, 199, shall be registered unless he has,-

(i) a paid-up equity capital of rupees one hundred crores, in case of a person carrying on the business of life insurance or general insurance; or

(ii) a paid-up equity capital of rupees two hundred crores, in case of a person carrying on exclusively the business as a reinsurer: Provided that in determining the paid-up equity capital specified under clause (i) or clause (ii), the deposit to be made under section 7 and any preliminary expenses incurred in the formation and registration of the company shall be excluded:

Provided further that an insurer carrying on business of life insurance, general insurance or re-insurance in India before the commencement of the Insurance Regulatory and Development Authority Act, 1999 and who is required to be registered under this Act, shall have a paid-up equity capital in accordance with clause (i) and clause (ii), as the case may be, within sex months of the commencement of that Act.

Deposits

Every insurer shall, in respect of the insurance business carried on by him in India, deposit and keep deposited with the Reserve Bank of India in one of the offices in India of the Bank for and on behalf of the Central Government the amount hereafter specified, either in cash or in approved securities estimated at the market value of the securities on the day of deposit, or partly in cash and partly in approved securities so estimated:-

(a) in the case of life insurance business, a sum equivalent to one per cent of his total gross premium written direct in India in any financial year commencing after the 31st day of March, 2000, not exceeding rupees ten crores;

(b) in the case of general insurance business, a sum equivalent to three per cent of his total gross premium written in India, in any financial year commencing after the 31st day of March, 2000, not exceeding rupees ten crores;

(c) in the case of re-insurance business, a sum of rupees twenty crores Provided that, where the business done or to be done is marine insurance only and relates exclusively to country craft or its cargo or both, the amount to be deposited under this sub-section shall be one hundred thousand rupees only: Provided further that in respect of an insurer not having a share capital and carrying on only such insurance business as in the opinion of the Central Government is not carried on ordinarily by insurers under separate policies, the Central Government may, by notification under Official Gazette, order that the provisions of this sub-section shall apply to such insurer with the modification that instead of sum of rupees twenty lakhs or rupees ten lakhs, as the case may be, the deposit to be made by such insurer shall be such amount, being not less than one hundred and fifty thousand rupees, as may be specified in the said order.

Audit

The balance-sheet, profit and loss account, revenue account and profit and loss appropriation account of every insurer, in the case of an insurer specified in sub-clause (a)(ii) or sub-clause (b) of clause (9) of section 2 in respect of all insurance business transacted by him, and in the case of any other insurer in respect of the insurance business transacted by him in India, shall, unless they are subject to audit under the Indian Companies Act, 1913 (7 of 1913), be audited annually by an auditor, and the auditor shall in the audit of all such accounts have the powers of, exercise the functions vested in, and discharge the duties and be subject to the liabilities and penalties imposed on, auditors of companies by section 145 of the Indian Companies Act, 1913.

This Act not to apply to preparation of account, etc., for periods prior to this Act coming into force.

Nothing in this Act shall apply to the preparation of accounts by an insurer and the audit and submission thereof in respect of any accounting year which has expired prior to the commencement of this Act, and notwithstanding the other provisions of this Act, such accounts shall be prepared, audited and submitted in accordance with the law in force immediately before the commencement of this Act.

Investment of Assets

(1) Every insurer shall invest and at all times keep invested assets equivalent to not less than the sum of-

(a) the amount of his liabilities to holders of life insurance policies in India on account of matured claims, and

(b) the amount required to meet the liability on policies of life insurance maturing for payment in India, less-

(i) the amount of premiums which have fallen due to the insurer on such policies but have not been paid and the days of grace for payment of which have not expired, and

(ii) any amount due to the insurer for loans granted on and within the surrender values of policies of life insurance maturing for payment in India issued by him or by an insurer whose business he has acquired and in respect of which he has assumed liability, in the manner following, namely, twenty-five per cent of the said sum in Government securities, a further sum equal to not less than twenty-five per cent of the said sum in Government securities or other approved securities and the balance in any of the approved investments specified in sub-section (1) of section 27A or, subject to the limitations, conditions and restrictions specified in sub-section (2) of that section, in any over investment.

(2) For the purposes of subsection (1),—

(a) the amount of any deposit made under section 7 or section 98 by the insurer in respect of his life insurance business shall be deemed to be assets invested or kept invested Government securities;

(b) The securities of, or guaranteed as to principal and interest by, the Government of the United Kingdom shall be regarded as approved securities other than Government securities for a period of four years from the commencement of the Insurance (Amendment) Act, 1950 (47 of 1950), in the manner and to the extent hereinafter specified, namely:—

(i) during the first year, to the extent of twenty-five per cent in value of the sum referred to in sub-section (1);

(ii) during the second year, to the extent of eighteen and three fourths per cent in value of the said sum;

(iii) during the third year, to the extent of twelve and a half per cent in value of the said sum; and

(iv) during the fourth year, to the extent of six and a quarter per cent in value of the said sum: Provided that, if the Authority so directs in any case, the securities specified in clause (b) shall be regarded as approved securities other than Government securities for a longer period than four years, but not exceeding six years in all and the manner in which and the extent to which the securities shall be so regarded shall be as specified in the direction;

(c) Any prescribed assets shall, subject to such conditions, if any, as may be prescribed, be deemed to be assets invested or kept invested in approved investments specified in sub-section (1) of section 27A.

(3) In computing the assets referred to in subsection (1),—

(a) any investment made with reference to any currency other than the Indian rupee which is in excess of the amount required to meet the liabilities of the insurer in India with reference to that currency, to the extent of such excess; and

(b) any investment made in the purchase of any immoveable property outside India or on the security of any such property, shall not be taken into account: Provided that nothing contained in this sub-section shall affect the operation of sub-section (2): Provided further that the Authority may, either generally or in any particular case, direct that any investment, whether made before or after the commencement of the Insurance (Amendment) Act, 1950 (47 of 1950), and whether made in or outside India, shall, subject to such conditions as may be imposed, be taken into account, in such manner as may be specified in computing the assets referred to in sub-section (1) and where any direction has been issued under this proviso copies thereof shall be laid before Parliament as soon as may be after it is issued.

(4) Where an insurer has accepted reassurance in respect of any policies of life insurance issued by another insurer and maturing for payment in India or has ceded reassurance to another insurer in respect of any such policies issued by himself, the sum referred to in subsection (1) shall be increased by the amount of the liability involved in such acceptance and decreased by the amount of the liability involved in such cession.

(5) The Government securities and other approved securities in which assets are under sub-section (1) to be invested and kept invested shall be held by the insurer free of any encumbrance, charge, hypothecation or lien.

(6) The assets required by this section to be held invested by an insurer incorporated or domiciled outside India shall, except to the extent of any part thereof which consists of foreign assets held outside India, be held in India and all such assets shall be held in trust for the discharge of the liabilities of the nature referred to in sub-section (1) and shall be vested in trustees resident in India and approved by the Authority, and the instrument of trust under this sub-section shall be executed by the insurer with the approval of the Authority and shall define the manner in which alone the subject-matter of the trust shall be dealt with.

Explanation.—This sub-section shall apply to an insurer-incorporated India whose share capital to the extent of one-third is owned by, or the members of whose governing body to the extent of one-third consists of, members domiciled elsewhere than in India.

Power to Appoint Staff

The Authority may appoint such staff, and at such places as it or he may consider necessary, for the scrutiny of the returns, statements and information furnished by insurers under this Act and generally to ensure the efficient performance of the functions of the Authority under this Act.

Registration of principal agents, chief agents and special agents

(1) The Authority or an officer authorized by it in this behalf shall in the prescribed manner and on payment of the prescribed fee, which shall not be more than twenty-five rupees for a principal agent or a chief

agent and ten rupees for a special agent, register any person who makes an application to him in the prescribed manner if,—

(a) in the case of an individual, he does not suffer from any of the disqualifications mentioned in sub-section (4) of Section 42, or

(b) in the case of a company or firm, any of its directors or partners does not suffer from any of the said disqualifications, and a certificate to Act as a principal agent, chief agent or special agent, as the case may be, for the purpose of procuring insurance business shall be issued to him.

(2) A certificate issued under this section shall entitle the holder thereof to act as a principal agent, chief agent, or special agent, as the case may be, for any insurer.

(3) A certificate issued under this section shall remain in force for a period of twelve months only from the date of issue, but shall, on application made on this behalf, be renewed from year to year on production of a certificate from the insurer concerned that the provisions of clauses (2) and (3) of Part A of the Sixth Schedule in the case of a principal agent, the provisions of clauses (2) and (4) of Part B of the said Schedule in the case of a chief agent, and the provisions of clauses (2) and (3) of Part C of the said Schedule in the case of a special agent, have been complied with, and on payment of the prescribed fee, which shall not be more than twenty-five rupees, in the case of a principal agent or a chief agent, and ten rupees in the case of a special agent, and an additional fee of the prescribed amount not exceeding five rupees by way of penalty, in cases where the application for renewal of the certificate does not reach the issuing authority before the date on which the certificate ceases to

remain in force: Provided that, where the applicant is an individual, he does not suffer from any of the disqualifications mentioned in clauses (b) to (d) of sub-section (4) of section 42 and where the applicant is a company or a firm, any of its directors or partners does not suffer from any of the said disqualifications.

(4) Where it is found that the principal agent, chief agent or special agent being an individual is, or being a company or firm contains a director or partner who is suffering from any of the disqualifications mentioned in subsection (4) of section 42, without prejudice to any other penalty to which he may be liable, the Authority shall, and where a principal agent, chief agent or special agent has contravened any of the provisions of this Act may cancel the certificate issued under this section to such principal agent, chief agent or special agent.

(5) The authority which issued any certificate under this section may issue a duplicate certificate to replace a certificate lost, destroyed or mutilated on payment of the prescribed fee, which shall not be more than two rupees.

(6) Any person who acts as a principal agent, chief agent or special agent, without holding a certificate issued under this section to act as such, shall be punishable with fine which may extend to five hundred rupees, and any insurer or any person acting on behalf of an insurer, who appoints as a principal agent, chief agent or special agent any person not entitled to act as such or transacts any insurance business in India through any such person, shall be punishable with fine which may extend to one thousand rupees.

(7) Where the person contravening sub-section (6) is a company or a firm, then, without prejudice to any

other proceedings which may be taken against the company or firm, every director, manager, secretary or any other officer of the company, and every partner of the firm who is knowingly a party to such contravention shall be punishable with fine which may extend to five hundred rupees.

(8) The provisions of sub-sections (6) and (7) shall not take effect until the expiry of six months from the commencement of the Insurance (Amendment) Act, 1950.

(9) No insurer shall, on or after the commencement of the Insurance (Amendment) Act, 2002, appointment or transacts any insurance business in India through any principal agent, chief agent or special agent.

Regulation of Employment of Principal Agents

(1) No insurer shall, after the expiration of seven years from the commencement of the Insurance (Amendment) Act, 1950, appoint, or transact any insurance business in India, through a principal agent.

(2) Every contract between an insurer and a principal agent shall be in writing and the terms contained in Part A of the Sixth Schedule shall be deemed to be incorporated in, and form part of, every such contract.

(3) No insurer shall, after the commencement of the Insurance (Amendment) Act, 1950 (47 of 1950), appoint any person as a principal agent except in a presidency-town unless the appointment is by way of renewal of any contract subsisting at such commencement.

(4) Within sixty days of the commencement of the Insurance (Amendment) Act, 1950 (47 of 1950), every principal agent shall file with the insurer concerned a full list of insurance agents employed by him indicating the terms of the contract between the principal agent and each of such insurance agents,

and, if any principal agent fails to file such a list within the period specified, any commission payable to such principal agent on premiums received from the date of expiry of the said period of sixty days until the date of the filing of the said list shall, notwithstanding anything in any contract to the contrary, cease to be so payable.

(5) A certified copy of every contract as is referred to in sub-section (2) shall be furnished by the insurer to the Authority within thirty days of his entering into such contract, and intimation of any change in any such contract shall be furnished by the insurer with full particulars thereof to the Authority within thirty days of the making of any such change.

(6) If the commission due to any insurance agent in respect of any general insurance business procured by such agent is not paid by the principal agent for any reason, the insurer may pay the insurance agent the commission so due and recover the amount so paid from the principal agent concerned.

(7) Every contract as is referred to in sub-section (2), subsisting at the commencement of the Insurance (Amendment) Act, 1950 (47 of 1950), shall, with respect to terms regarding remuneration, be deemed to have been so altered as to be in accordance with the provisions of sub-section (4) of section 40A.

(8) If any dispute arises as to whether a person is or was a principal agent the matter shall be referred to the Authority, whose decision shall be final.

(9) Every insurer shall maintain a register in which the name and address of every principal agent appointed by him, the date of such appointment and the date, if any, on which the appointment ceased shall be entered.

Commission, Brokerage or Fee Payable to Intermediary or Insurance Intermediary

(1) No intermediary or insurance intermediary shall be paid or contract to be paid by way of commission, fee or as remuneration in any form, an amount exceeding thirty per cent of the premium payable as may be specified by the regulations made by the Authority, in respect of any policy or policies effected through him: Provided that the Authority may specify different amounts payable by way of commission, fee or as remuneration to an intermediary or insurance intermediary or different classes of business of insurance.

(2) Without prejudice to the provisions contained in this Act, the Authority may, by the regulations made in this behalf, specify the requirements of capital, form of business and other conditions to act as an intermediary or insurance intermediary.

Register of Insurance Agents

Every insurer and every person who acting on behalf of an insurer employs insurance agents shall maintain a register showing the name and address of every insurance agent appointed by him and the date on which his appointment began and the date, if any, on which his appointment ceased.

IRDA ACT 1999

The Insurance Act, 1938 had provided for setting up of the Controller of Insurance to act as a strong and powerful supervisory and regulatory authority for insurance. Post nationalization, the role of Controller of Insurance diminished considerably in significance since the insurance companies were owned by the Government.

With the opening up of the insurance industry to the private sector, the need for a strong, independent and autonomous Insurance Regulatory Authority was felt. As the enacting of legislation would have taken time, the then Government constituted through a Government resolution an Interim Insurance Regulatory Authority pending the enactment of a comprehensive legislation. The Insurance Regulatory and Development Authority Act, 1999 is an act to provide for the establishment of an Authority to protect the interests of holders of insurance policies, to regulate, promote and ensure orderly growth of the insurance industry and for matters connected therewith or incidental thereto and further to amend the Insurance Act, 1938, the Life Insurance Corporation Act, 1956 and the General insurance Business (Nationalization) Act, 1972 to end the monopoly of the Life Insurance Corporation of India (for life insurance business) and General Insurance Corporation and its subsidiaries (for general insurance business).

Extent and Commencement

- This Act may be called the Insurance Regulatory and Development Authority Act, 1999.
- The act extends to the whole of India and will come into force on such date as the Central Government may, by notification in the Official Gazette specify. Different dates may be appointed for different provisions of this Act.
- The Act has defined certain terms, some of the most important ones are as follows:-
- Appointed day means the date on which the Authority is established under the act.
- Authority means the established under this Act.

With effect from such date as the Central Government may, by notification, appoint the Insurance Regulatory and Develop is to be constituted. The Authority shall be a body corporate, having perpetual succession and a common seal with power, subject to the provisions of this Act, to acquire, hold and dispose of property, and to contract and can be sue or be sued in its own name. The head office of the Authority shall be at such place as the Central Government may decide from time to time and it may establish offices at other places in India.

Composition of Authority

The Authority shall consist of the following members, namely:

(a) a Chairperson;

(b) not more than five whole-time members;

(c) not more than four part-time members, to be appointed by the Central Government from amongst persons of ability, integrity and standing who have knowledge or experience in life insurance, general insurance, actuarial science, finance, economics, law, accountancy, administration or any other discipline which would, in the opinion of the Central Government, be useful to the Authority:

The Central Government while appointing the Chairperson and the whole-time members must ensure that at least one person each is a person having knowledge or experience in life insurance, general insurance or actuarial science respectively.

Tenure of office of Chairperson and other members The Chairperson and every other whole-time member shall hold office for a term of five years from the date on which he enters upon his office and shall be eligible for reappointment: However, no person shall hold office as such Chairperson after he has attained the age of sixty-five years and no person shall hold office as such whole-time member after he has attained the age of sixty-two years. A part-time member shall hold office for a term not exceeding five years from the date on which he enters upon his office.

A member may:-

(a) relinquish his office by giving in writing to the Central Government notice of not less than three months; or be removed from his office in accordance with the following provisions.

Removal from Office

The Central Government may remove from office any member who:-

(a) is, or at any time has been, adjudged as insolvent;

(b) has become physically or mentally incapable of acting as a member;

(c) has been convicted of any offence which, in the opinion of the Central Government, involves moral turpitude;

(d) has acquired such financial or other interest as is likely to affect prejudicially his functions as a member;

(e) has so abused his position as to render his continuation in office detrimental to the public interest.

No such member shall be removed under clause (d) or clause (e) unless he has been given a reasonable opportunity of being heard in the matter. Salary and allowances of Chairperson and members The salary and allowances payable to, and other terms and conditions of service of, the members other than part-time members shall be such as may be prescribed. The part-time members shall receive such allowances as may be prescribed. The salary, allowances and other conditions of service of a member shall not be varied to his disadvantage after appointment.

Bar on Future Employment of Members

The Chairperson and the whole-time members shall not, for a period of two years from the date on which they cease to hold office as such, except with the previous approval of the Central Government, accept:-

(a) any employment either under the Central Government or under any State Government; or

(b) any appointment in any company in the Insurance sector.

Administrative powers of Chairperson

The Chairperson shall have the powers of general superintendence and direction in respect of all administrative matters of the Authority.

Meeting of Authority

The Authority shall meet at such times and places, and shall observe such rules and procedures in regard to transaction of business at its meetings (including quorum at such meetings) as may be determined by regulations.

The Chairperson, or if for any reason he is unable to attend a meeting of the Authority, any other member chosen by the members present from amongst themselves at the meeting shall preside at the meeting. All questions which come up before any meeting of the Authority shall be decided by a majority vote of the members present and voting, and in the event of equality of votes, the Chairperson, or in his absence, the person presiding shall have a second or casting vote. The Authority may make regulations for the transaction of business at its meetings.

Vacancies, etc., not to Invalidate Proceedings of Authority

No Act or proceeding of the Authority shall be invalid merely by reason of:-

(a) any vacancy in, or any defect in the constitution of, the Authority;

(b) any defect in the appointment of a person acting as a member of the Authority;

(c) any irregularity in the procedure of the Authority not affecting the merits of the case.

Officers and Employees of Authority

The Authority may appoint officers and such other employees, as it considers necessary for the efficient discharge of its functions under this Act. The terms and other conditions of service of officers and other employees of the Authority shall be governed by regulations made under this Act.

Transfer of Assets, Liabilities, etc, of the Interim Insurance Regulatory

Authority will be transferred to the Authority on the appointed day. All suits and other legal proceedings instituted or which could have been instituted by or against the Interim Insurance Regulatory Authority immediately before that day may be continued or may be instituted by or against the Authority.

Duties, Powers and Functions of Authority

Subject to the provisions of this Act and any other law for the time being in force, the Authority has the duty to regulate, promote and ensure orderly growth of the insurance business and re-insurance business. The powers and functions of the Authority include:-

(a) to issue to the applicant a certificate of registration, to renew, modify, withdraw, suspend or cancel such registration

(b) protection of the interests of the policy-holders in matters concerning assigning of policy, nomination by policy-holders, insurable interest, settlement of insurance claim, surrender value of policy, and other terms and conditions of contracts of insurance

(c) specifying requisite qualifications code of conduct and practical training for intermediary or insurance intermediaries and agents

(d) specifying the code of conduct for surveyors and loss assessors

(e) promoting efficiency in the conduct of insurance business

(f) promoting and regulating professional organizations connected with the insurance and reinsurance business

(g) levying fees and other charges for carrying out the purposes of this Act

(h) calling for information from, undertaking inspection of, conducting enquiries and investigations including audit of the insurers, intermediaries, insurance intermediaries and other organizations connected with the insurance business

(i) control and regulation of the rates, advantages, terms and conditions that may be offered by insurers in respect of general insurance business not so controlled and regulated by the Tariff Advisory Committee under section 64U of the Insurance Act, 1938

(j) prescribing the form and manner in which books of account shall be maintained and statement of accounts will be rendered by insurers and other insurance intermediaries

(k) Regulating investment of funds by insurance companies

(l) regulating maintenance of margin of solvency

(m) adjudication of disputes between insurers and intermediaries or insurance intermediaries

(n) supervising the functioning of the Tariff Advisory Committee

(o) specifying the percentage of premium income of the insurer to finance schemes for promoting and regulating professional organizations

(p) specifying the percentage of life insurance business and general insurance business to be undertaken by the insurer in the rural or social sector

(q) exercising such other powers as may be prescribed

Finance, Accounts and Audit

Grants by Central Government

The Central Government may, after due appropriation made by the Parliament by law in this behalf, make to the Authority grants of such sums of money as the Government may think fit for being utilized for the purposes of this Act.

Fund

A Fund to be called "The Insurance Regulatory and Development Authority Fund" is to be established and the following sums will be credited thereto:-

(a) all Government grants, fees and charges received by the Authority

(b) all sums received by the Authority from such other source as may be decided upon by the Central Government

(c) the percentage of prescribed income received from the insurer.

The Fund shall be applied for meeting the following expenses:-

(a) the salaries, allowances and other remuneration of the members, officers and other employees of the Authority

(b) the other expenses of the Authority in connection with the discharge of its functions and for the purposes of this Act.

Accounts and Audit

The Authority shall maintain proper accounts and other relevant records and prepare an annual statement of accounts in such form as may be prescribed by the Central Government in consultation with the Comptroller and Auditor General of India.

The accounts of the Authority shall be audited by the Comptroller and Auditor General of India at such intervals as may be specified by him and any expenditure incurred in connection with such audit shall be payable by the Authority to the Comptroller and Auditor General of India. The Comptroller and Auditor-General of India and other person appointed by him in connection with the audit of the accounts of the Authority shall have the same rights and privileges and authority in connection with such audit as the Comptroller and Auditor General generally has in connection with the audit of the Government accounts and, in particular, shall have the right to demand the production of books, accounts, connected vouchers and other documents and papers and to inspect any of the officers of the Authority. The accounts of the Authority as certified by the Comptroller and Auditor General of India or any other person appointed by him in this behalf together with the audit report thereon shall be forwarded annually to the Central Government and that Government shall cause the same to be laid before each House of Parliament.

Powers of Central Government

The Authority shall, in exercise of its powers or the performance of its functions under this Act, be bound by such directions on questions of policy, other than those relating to technical and administrative matters, as the Central Government may give in writing to it from time to time However, Authority must, as far as practicable, be given an opportunity to express its views before any such direction is given. The decision of the Central Government, whether a question is one of policy or not, shall be final. Power of Central Government to supersede Authority If at any time the Central Government is of the opinion:-

(a) that, on account of circumstances beyond the control of the Authority, it is unable to discharge the functions or perform the duties imposed on it by or under the provisions of this Act: or

(b) that the Authority has persistently defaulted in complying with any direction given by the Central Government under this Act or in the discharge of the functions or performance of the duties imposed on it by or under the provisions of this Act and as a result of such default the financial position of the Authority or the administration of the Authority has suffered; or

(c) that circumstances exist which render in necessary in the public interest so to do, the Central Government may, by notification and for reasons to be specified therein, supersede the Authority for such period, not exceeding six months, as may be specified in the notification and appoint a person to be the Controller of Insurance. However, before issuing any such notification, the Central Government shall give a reasonable opportunity to the Authority to make representations against the proposed supersession and shall consider the representations, if any, of the Authority.

Upon the publication of such notification superseding the Authority:-

(a) the Chairperson and other members shall, as from the date of supersession, vacate their offices as such;

(b) all the powers, functions and duties which may, by or under the provisions of this Act, be exercised or discharged by or on behalf of the Authority shall, until the Authority is reconstituted, be exercised and discharged by the Controller of Insurance; and

(c) all properties owned or controlled by the Authority shall, until the Authority is reconstituted vest in the Central Government.

On or before the expiration of the period of supersession specified in such a notification, the Central Government shall reconstitute the Authority by a fresh appointment of its Chairperson and other members and in such case any person who had vacated his office under the notification shall not be deemed disqualified for reappointment.

The Central Government shall cause a copy of the notification issued and a full report of any action taken under this section and the circumstances leading to such action to be laid before each House of Parliament at the earliest.

Furnishing of Eeturns, etc., to the Central Government

The Authority must furnish to the Central Government at such time and in such form and manner as may be prescribed, or as the Central Government may direct, such returns and statements and such particulars in regard to any proposed or existing programme for the promotion and development of the insurance industry as the Central Government may, from time to time, require.

The Authority must, within nine months after the close of each financial year, submit to the Central Government a report giving a true and full account of its activities including the activities for promotion and development of the insurance business during the previous financial year. Copies of the reports must be laid, as soon as may be after they are received, before each House of Parliament. Chairperson, members, officers and employees of Authority to be public servants.

The Chairperson, members, officers and other employees of the Authority shall be deemed, when acting or purporting to act in pursuance of any of the provisions of this Act, to be public servants within the meaning of section 21 of the Indian Penal Code.

Protection of Action taken in Good Faith

No suit, prosecution or other legal proceedings shall lie against the Central Government or any officer of the Central Government or any member, officer or other employee of the Authority for anything which is in good faith done or intended to be done under this Act or the rules or regulations made there under. However, nothing in this Act exempts any person from any suit or other proceedings which might, apart from this Act, be brought against him.

Delegation of Powers

The Authority may, by general or special order in writing, delegate to the Chairperson or any other member or officer of the Authority, subject to such conditions, if any, as may be specified in the order such of its powers and functions under this Act as it may deem necessary.

The Authority may, by a general or special order in writing, also form Committees of the members and delegate to them the powers and functions of the Authority as may be specified by the regulations.

Power to make Rules

The Central Government may, by notification, make rules for carrying out the purposes of this Act. Such rules may provide for all or any of the following matters, namely:-

(a) the salary and allowances payable to and other conditions of service of the members other than part-time members

(b) the allowances to be paid to the part-time members

(c) such other powers that may be performed by the Authority

(d) the form of annual statement of accounts to be prepared by the Authority

(e) the time at, the form and the manner in which returns and statements and particulars are to be furnished to the Central Government

(f) the matters on which the Insurance Advisory Committee shall advise the authority

(g) any other matter which is to be, or may be, prescribed, or in respect of which provision is to be or may be made by rules.

Establishment of Insurance Advisory Committee

The Authority may, by notification, establish with effect from such date as it may specify in such notification, a Committee to be known as the Insurance Advisory Committee. The Insurance Advisory Committee shall consist of not more than twenty-five members excluding ex officio members to represent the interests of commerce, industry, transport, agriculture, consumer fora, surveyors, agents, intermediaries, organizations engaged in safety and loss prevention, research bodies and employees' association in the insurance sector. The Chairperson and the members of the Authority shall be the ex officio Chairperson and ex officio members of the Insurance Advisory Committee. The objects of the Insurance Advisory committee shall be to advise the Authority on matters relating to the making of the regulations. The Insurance Advisory Committee may advise the Authority on such other matters as may be prescribed.

Capital Requirements

Requirement as to Capital

No insurer carrying on the business of life insurance, general insurance, or reinsurance in India on or after the commencement of the Insurance Regulatory and Development Authority Act, 1999, shall be registered unless he has:-

1. a paid-up equity capital of rupees one hundred crores, in case of a person carrying on the business of life insurance or general insurance; or

2. a paid-up equity capital of rupees two hundred crores, in case of a person carrying on exclusively the business as a reinsurer:

In determining the paid-up equity capital specified under clause (i) or clause (ii), the deposit to be made under section 7 and any preliminary expenses incurred in the formation and registration of the company shall be excluded: An insurer carrying on business of life insurance, general insurance or reinsurance in India before the commencement of the Insurance Regulatory and Development Authority Act, 1999 and who is required to be registered under this Act, shall have a paid-up equity capital in accordance with clause (i) and clause (ii), as the case may be, within six months of the commencement of that Act.

Where, the nominal value of the shares intended to be transferred by any individual, firm, group, constituents of a group, or body corporate under the same management, jointly or severally exceeds one per cent. Of paid up capital of the insurer, previous approval of the Authority must be obtained for the transfer. Explanation.-For the purpose of this sub-clause, the expressions "group" and "same management", shall have the same meanings respectively assigned to them in the Monopolies and Restrictive Trade Practices Act, 1969.

The following sections have been inserted:-

Provisions of investment of funds outside India.

No insurer shall directly or indirectly invest outside India, the funds of the policyholders.

Manner and Conditions of Investment

The Authority may, in the interests of the policyholders, specify by regulations made by the Authority, the time, manner and other conditions of investment of assets to be held by an insurer for the purposes of this Act.

The Authority may, after taking into account the nature of business and to protect the interests of the policyholders, issue to an insurer the directions relating to the time, manner, and other conditions of investment of assets to be held by him. However, no directions shall be issued unless the insurer concerned has been given a reasonable opportunity of being heard.

Insurance Business in Rural or Social Sector

Every insurer shall, after the commencement of the Insurance Regulatory and Development Authority Act, 1999, undertake such percentages of life insurance business and general insurance business in the rural or social sector, as may be specified, in the Official Gazette by the Authority, in this behalf.

Miscellaneous Provisions

Penalty for default in complying with, or act in contravention of, this Act. lf any person, who is required under this Act, or rules or regulations made there under,-

(a) to furnish any document, statement, account, return or report to the Authority, fail to furnish the same; or

(b) to comply with the directions, fails to comply with such directions;

(c) to maintain solvency margin, fails to maintain such solvency margin;

(d) to comply with the directions on the insurance treaties, fails to comply with sue directions on the insurance treaties, he shall be liable to a penalty not exceeding five lakhs rupees for each such failure and punishable with fine.

lf a person makes a statement, or furnishes any document, statement, account, return or report which is false and which he either knows or believes to be false or does not believe to be true:

(a) he shall be liable to a penalty not exceeding five lakhs rupees for each such failure; and

(b) he shall be punishable with imprisonment which may extend to three years or with fine for each such failure.

If any director, managing director, manager or to~ officer or employees of an insurer wrongfully obtains possession of any property or wrongfully applies to any purpose of the Act, he shall be liable to a penalty not exceeding two lakhs rupees for each such failure.

Offences by companies, Where any offence under this Act has been committed by a company, every person who, at the time the offence was committed, was in charge of, and was responsible to, the Company for the conduct of the business of the company as well as the company shall be deemed to be guilty of the offence and shall be liable to be proceeded against and punished accordingly: Nothing contained in this sub-section shall render any such person liable to any punishment, if he proves that the offence was committed without his knowledge or that he had exercised all due diligence to prevent the commission of such offence. Where any offence under this Act has been committed by a company and it is proved that the offence has been committed with the consent or connivance of, or is attributable to any neglect on the part of, any director, manager, secretary or other officer of the company, such director, manager, secretary or other officer shall be deemed to be guilty of that offence and shall be liable to be proceeded against and punished accordingly.

Explanation: For the purposes of this section,-

(a) "company" means any body corporate, and includes a firm, an association of person or a body of individuals whether incorporated or not; and

(b) "director", in relation to-

(i) a firm means a partner in the firm;

(ii) an association of persons or a body of individuals, means any-member controlling the affairs thereof.

Power of Authority to make regulations.

The Authority may, by notification in the Official Gazette, make regulations consistent with this Act and the rules made there under, to carry out the provisions of this Act.

AGENCY LAW

At times all of us act as principals and agents. If I my friend ask me to deposit his water bill, then he is acting as principal and I am as agent. Agency Law is contained in Chapter X {Secs182 to 238} of the Indian Contact Act 1872. "Agent" and "principal": An "agent" is a person employed to do any act for another, or to represent another in dealings with third persons. The person for whom such act is done, or represented, is called the "principal". {sec182}.

Who may employ agent: Any person who is of the age of majority according to the law to which he is subject, and who is of sound mind, may employ an agent. Who may be an agent: As between the principal and third persons, any person may become an agent, but no person who is not of the age of majority and sound mind can become an agent, so as to be responsible to the principal according to the provisions in that behalf herein contained.

Consideration not necessary: No consideration is necessary to create an agency. Agent's authority may be express or implied: The authority of an agent may be express or implied.

Definitions of express and implied authority: An authority is said to be express when it is given by words spoken or written. An authority is said to be implied when it is to be inferred from the circumstances of the case; and things spoken or written, or the ordinary course of dealing, may be accounted circumstances of the case.

Illustration

Aman owns a shop in Serampur, living himself in Calcutta, and visiting the shop occasionally. Bharat manages the shop, and he is in the habit of ordering goods from Chaman in the name of Aman for the purposes of the shop, and of paying for them out of Aman's funds with Aman's knowledge.

Bharat has an implied authority from Aman to order goods from Chaman in the name of Aman for the purpose of the shop. Extent of agent's authority: An agent, having an authority to do an act, has authority to do every lawful thing, which is necessary in order to do such act. An agent having an authority to carry on a business has authority to do every lawful thing necessary for the purpose, or usually done in the course, of conducting such business.

Illustrations

(a) A is employed by B, residing in London, to recover at Bombay a debt due to B. A may adopt any legal process necessary for the purpose of recovering the debt, and may give a valid discharge for the same.

(b) A constitutes B his agent to carry on his business of a shipbuilder. B may purchase timber and other materials, and hire workmen, for the purpose of carrying on the business.

Agent's Authority in an Emergency: An agent has authority, in an emergency, to do all such acts for the purpose of protecting his principal from loss and would be done by a person or ordinary prudence, in his own case, under similar circumstances.

SUB AGENT

When Agent cannot Delegate

An agent cannot lawfully employ another to perform acts, which he has expressly, or impliedly undertaken to perform personally, unless by the ordinary custom of trade a sub-agent may, or, from the nature of agency, a sub-agent must, be employed.

"Sub-agent" Defined

A "sub-agent" is a person employed by, and acting under the control of, the original agent in the business of the agency.

Representation of Principal by Sub-agent Properly Appointed

Where a sub-agent is properly appointed, the principal is, so far as regards third persons, represented by the sub-agent, and is bound by and responsible for his acts, as if he were an agent originally appointed by the principal. Agent's responsibility for sub-agents: The agent is responsible to the principal for the acts of the sub-agent.

Sub-agent's responsibility: The sub-agent is responsible for his acts to the agent, but not to the principal, except in case of fraud or willful wrong.

Agent's Responsibility for Sub-agent Appointed without Authority

Where an agent, without having authority to do so, has appointed a person to act as a sub-agent, the agent stands towards such person in the relation of a principal to an agent, and is responsible for his acts both to the principal and to third person; the principal is not represented, by or responsible for the acts of the person so employed, nor is that person responsible to the principal. Relation between principal and person duly appointed by agent to act in business of agency When an agent, holding an express or implied authority to name another person to act for the principal in the business of the agency, has named another person accordingly, such person is not a sub-agent, but an agent of the principal for such part of the business of the agency as is entrusted to him.

Agent's Duty in Naming such Person

In selecting such agent for his principal, an agent is bound to exercise the same amount of discretion as a man of ordinary prudence would exercise in his own case; and, if he does this, he is not responsible to the principal for the acts of negligence of the agent so selected.

Illustrations

A instructs B, a merchant, to buy a ship for him. B employs a ship-surveyor of good reputation to choose a ship for A. The surveyor makes the choice negligently and the ship turns out to be unseaworthy and is lost. B is not, but the surveyor is, responsible to A. Right of person as to acts done for him without his authority-effect of ratification

Where acts are done by one person on behalf of another, but without his knowledge or authority, he may elect to ratify or to disown such acts. If he ratifies them, the same effects will follow as if they had been performed by his authority. Ratification may be expressed or implied

Ratification may be expressed or may be implied in the conduct of the person on whose behalf the acts are done.

Illustrations

(a) A, without authority, buys goods, for B. Afterwards B sells them to C on his own account; B's conduct implies a ratification of the purchase made for him by A.

(b) A, without B's authority, lends B's money to C. Afterwards B accepts interest on the money from C. B's conduct implies a ratification of the loan. Knowledge requisite for valid ratification

No valid ratification can be made by a person whose knowledge of the facts of the case is materially defective.

Effect of ratifying unauthorized act forming part of a transaction

A person ratifying any unauthorized act done on his behalf ratifies the whole of the transaction of which such act formed a part.

Ratification of Unauthorized act cannot Injure Third Person

An act done by one person on behalf of another, without such other person's authority, which, if done with authority would have the effect of subjecting a third person to damages, or of terminating any right to interest of a third person cannot, by ratification, be made to have such effect.

REVOCATION OF AUTHORITY

Termination of Agency

An agency is terminated by the principal revoking his authority, or by the agent renouncing the business of the agency; or by the business of the agency being completed; or by either the principal or agent dying or becoming of unsound mind; or by the principal being adjudicated an insolvent under the provisions of any Act for the time being in force for the relief of insolvent debtors. Termination of agency, where agent has an interest in subject-matter Where the agent has himself an interest in the property, which forms the subject matter of the agency, the agency cannot, in the absence of an express contract, be terminated to the prejudice of such interest.

Illustration

A, gives authority to B to sell A's land, and to pay himself, out of the proceeds, the debts due to him from A.A cannot revoke this authority, nor can it be terminated by his insanity or death.

When principal may revoke agent's authority.

The principal may, save as is otherwise provided by the last preceding section, revoke the authority given to his agent at any time before the authority has been exercised, so as to bind the principal.

Revocation where authority has been partly exercised.

The principal cannot revoke the authority given to his agent after the authority has been partly exercised; so far as regards such acts and obligations as arise from acts already done in the agency. Compensation for revocation by principal, or renunciation by agent. Where there is an express or implied contract that the agency should be continued for any period of time, the principal must make compensation to the agent, or the agent to the principal, as the case may be, for any previous revocation or renunciation of the agency without sufficient cause.

Notice of revocation or renunciation.

Reasonable notice must be given of such revocation or renunciation, otherwise the damage thereby resulting to the principal or the agent, as the case may be, must be made good to the one by the other.

Revocation and renunciation may be expressed or implied.

Revocation or renunciation may be expressed or may be implied in the conduct of that principal or agent respectively.

Illustration

A empowers B to let A's house. Afterwards A lets it himself. This is an implied revocation of B's authority.

When termination of agent's authority takes effect as to agent, and as to third persons.

The termination of the authority of an agent does not, so far as regards the agent, take effect before it becomes known to him, or, so far as regards third persons, before it becomes known to them.

Agent's duty on termination of agency by principal's death or insanity When an agency is terminated by the principal dying or becoming of unsound mind, the agent is bound to take on behalf of the representative, of his late principal, all reasonable steps for the protection and reservation of the interests entrusted to him.

Termination of Sub-agent's Authority

The termination of the authority of an agent causes the termination (subject to the rules herein contained regarding the termination of an agent's authority) of the authority of all sub-agents appointed by him.

AGENT'S DUTY TO PRINCIPAL

Agent's Duty in Conducting Principal's Business

An agent is bound to conduct the business of his principal according to the directions given by the principal, or in the absence of any such directions according to the customs, which prevails in doing business of the same kind at the place where the agent conducts such business. When the agent acts otherwise, if any loss be sustained, he must make it good to his principal and if any profit accrues, he must account for it.

Skill and Diligence required from Agent

An agent is bound to conduct the business of the agency with as much skill as is generally possessed by person engaged in similar business unless the principal has notice of his want of skill.

The agent is always bound to act with reasonable diligence, and to use such skill as he possesses; and to make compensation to his principal in respect of the direct consequences of his own neglect, want of skill, or misconduct, but not in respect of loss or damage which are indirectly or remotely caused by such neglect, want of skill, or misconduct.

Agent's Accounts

An agent is bound to render proper accounts to his principal on demand. Agent's, duty to communicate with principal

It is the duty of an agent in case of difficulty, to use all reasonable diligence in communicating with his principal, and in seeking to obtain his instructions. Right of principal when agent deals, on his own account, in business of agency without principal's consent

If an agent deals on his own account in the business of the agency, without first obtaining the consent of his principal and acquainting him with all material circumstances, which have come to his own knowledge on the subject, the principal may

Repudiate the transaction, if the case shows, either that any material fact has been dishonestly concealed from him by the agent, or that the dealings of the agent have been disadvantageous to him.

Illustrations

(a) A direct B to sell A's estate. B buys the estate for himself in the name of C. A, on discovering that B has bought the estate for himself, may repudiate the sale, if he can show that B has dishonestly concealed any material fact, or that the seals has been disadvantageous to him.

(b) A directs B to sell A's estate. B, on looking over the estate before selling it, finds a mine on the estate which is unknown to A. B informs A that he wished to buy the estate for himself but conceals the discovery of the mine. A allows B to buy, in ignorance of the existence of the mine. A, on discovering that B knew of the mine at the time he bought the estate, may either repudiate or adopt the sale at his option.

Principal's right to benefit gained by agent dealing on his own account in business of agency.

If an agent, without the knowledge of his principal, deals in the business of the agency on his own account instead of on account to his principal, the principal is entitled to claim from the agent any benefit which may have resulted to him from the transaction. Agent's right of retainer out of sums received on principal's account An agent may retain, out of any sums received on account of the principal in the business of the agency, all moneys due to himself in respect of advances made or expenses properly incurred by him in conducting such business, and also such remuneration as may be payable to him for acting as agent.

Agent's Duty to Pay sums received for Principal

Subject to such deductions, the agent is bound to pay to his principal all sums received on his account.

When agent's remuneration becomes due.

In the absence of any special contract, payment for the performance of any act is not due to the agent until the completion of such act; but an agent may detain moneys received by him on account of goods sold, although the whole of the goods consigned to him for sale may not have been sold, or although the sale may not be actually complete. Agent not entitled to remuneration for business misconduct.

An agent, who is guilty of misconduct in the business of the agency, is not entitled to any remuneration in respect of that part of the business, which he has misconducted.

Illustrations

A employs B to recover 1,000 rupees from C. Through B's misconduct the money is not recovered. B is entitled to no remuneration for his services and must make good the loss.

Agent's Lien on Principal's Property

In the absence of any contract to the contrary, an agent is entitled to retain goods, papers, and other property, whether movable or immovable of the principal received by him, until the amount due to himself for commission, disbursements and services in respect of the same has been paid or accounted for to him.

PRINCIPAL'S DUTY TO AGENT

Agent to be indemnified against consequences of lawful acts The employer of an agent is bound to indemnify him against the consequences of all lawful acts done by such agent in exercise of the authority conferred upon him.

Agent to be indemnified against consequences of acts done in good faith Where one person employs another to do an act, and the agent does the act in good faith, the employer is liable to indemnify the agent against the consequences of that act, though it may cause an injury to the rights of third persons. Non-liability of employer of agent to do a criminal act Where one person employees another to do an act which is criminal, the employer is not liable to the agent, either upon an express or an implied promise to indemnify him against the consequences of that Act.

Illustrations

A employs B to beat C, and agrees to indemnify him against all consequences of the act. B thereupon beats C, and has to pay damages to C for so doing. A is not liable to indemnify B for those damages. Compensation to agent for injury caused by principal's neglect. The principal must make compensation to his agent in respect of injury caused to such agent by the principal's neglect or want of skill.

Illustration

A employs B as a bricklayer in building a house, and put up the scaffolding himself. The scaffolding is unskillfully put up, and B is in consequence hurt. A must make compensation to B.

EFFECT OF AGENCY ON CONTRACTS WITH THIRD PERSONS

Enforcement and Consequences of Agent's Contract

Contracts entered into through an agent, and obligations arising from acts done by an agent, may be enforced in the same manner, and will have the same legal consequences as if the contracts had been entered into the acts done by the principal in person.

Illustrations

(a) A buys goods from B, knowing that he is an agent for their sale, but not knowing who the principal is. B's principal is the person entitled to claim from A the price of the goods, and A cannot, in a suit by the principal, set-off against that claim a debt due to himself from B.

(b) A, being B's agent; with authority to receive money on his behalf, receives from C a sum of money due to B. C is discharged of his obligation to pay the sum in question to B.

Principal how far Bound, when Agent exceeds Authority

When an agent does more than he is authorized to do, and when the part of what he does, which is within his authority, can be separated from the part, which is beyond his authority, so much only of what he does as is within his authority is binding as between him and his principal.

Principal not bound when excess of agent's authority is not separable Where an agent does more than he is authorized to do, and what he does beyond the scope of his authority cannot be separated from what is within it, the principal is not bound to recognize the transaction.

Illustration

A authorizes B to buy 500 sheep for him. B buys 500 sheep and 200 lambs for a sum of 6,000 rupees. A may repudiate the whole transaction.

Consequences of Notice given to Agent

Any notice given to or information obtained by the agent, provided it be given or obtained in the course of the business transacted by him for the principal, shall, as between the principal and third parties, have the same legal consequences as if it had been given to or obtained by the principal.

Illustrations

A is employed by B to buy from C goods of which C is the apparent owner. A was, before he was so employed a servant of C, and then learnt that the goods really belonged to D, but B is ignorant of that fact. In spite of the knowledge of his agent, B may set-off against the price of the goods a debt owing to him from C. Agent cannot personally enforce, nor be bound by, contracts on behalf of principal.

In the absence of any contract to that effect an agent cannot personally enforce contracts entered into by him on behalf of his principal, nor is he personally bound by them.

Presumption of contract to the contrary: Such a contract shall be presumed to exit in the following cases-

(1) Where the contract is made by an agent for the sa or purchase of goods for a merchant resident abroa

(2) Where agent does not disclose the name of hi principal;

(3) Where the principal, though disclosed, cannot be sued

Right of Parties to a Contract made by Agent not Disclosed

If an agent makes a contract with a person who neither, knows nor has reason to suspect, that he is an agent, his principal may require the performance of the contract; but the other contracting party has, as against the principal, the same right as he would have had as against if the agent had been the principal. If the principal discloses himself before the contract is completed, the other contracting party may refuse to fulfill the contract, if he can show that, if he had known who was the principal in the contract, or if he had known that the agent was not a principal, he would not have entered into the contract.

Performance of Contract with Agent Supposed to be Principal

Where one man makes a contract with another, neither knowing nor having reasonable ground to suspect that the other is an agent, the principal, if he requires the performance of the contract, can only obtain such performance subject to the right and obligations subsisting between the agent and the other party of the contract. Liability of principal inducing belief that agent's unauthorized acts were authorized.

When an agent has, without authority, done acts or incurred obligations to third person on behalf of his principal, the principal is bound by such acts or obligations, if he has by his word or conduct induced such third person to believe that such acts and obligations were within the scope of the agent's authority.

Illustrations

(a) A consigns goods to B for sale, and gives him instructions not to sell under a fixed price. C, being ignorant of B's instruction, enters into a contract with B to buy the goods at a price lower than the reserved price. A is bound by the contract

(b) A entrusts B with negotiable instruments endorsed in blank. B sells them to C in violation of private order from A. The sale is good.

Effect, on agreement, of misrepresentation or fraud by agent.

Misrepresentation made or fraud committed, by agent acting in the course of their business for their principals, have the same effect on agreements made by such agents as if such misrepresentations of frauds had been made or committed by the principals; but misrepresentations made, or frauds committed, by agents, in matters which do not affect their authority, do not affect their principals

Illustrations

(a) A, being B's agent for the sale of goods, induces C to buy them by a misrepresentation, which he was not authorized by B to make. The contract is voidable, as between B and C, at the option of C.

(c) A, the captain of B's ship, signs bills of lading without having received on board the goods mentioned therein. The bills of lading are void as between B and the pretended consignor.

CONSUMER PROTECTION ACT, 1986

The Consumer Protection Act was passed by the Parliament in 1986 and it came into force from 1987. Its purposes to protect consumers against defective goods, unsatisfactory services, unfair trade practices, etc. The Act provides for three-tier machinery consisting of District Forum, State Commission and National Commission.

It also provides for the formation protection councils in every state. The consumers can file their complaints at the appropriate forum for quick redressal. The complaint may relate to defective refrigerator or TV set, nonfunctional telephone, lack of due cares in medical treatment and so on. Any service or product given free of charge is not covered by the Act.

Definitions of Important Terms

Before studying the provisions of the CPA, it is necessary to understand the terms used in the Act. Let us understand some of the more important definitions. Complainant means:-

1. A consumer; or
2. Any voluntary consumer association registered under the Companies Act, 1956 or under any other law for the time being in force; or
3. The Central Government or any State Government, who or which makes a complaint; or
4. One or more consumers where there are numerous consumers having the same interest

Complaint means any allegation in writing made by a complainant that:-

1. an unfair trade practice or a restricted trade practice has been adopted by any trader
2. the goods bought by him or agreed to be bought by him suffer from one more defects
3. the services hired or availed of or agreed to be hired or availed of by him suffer from deficiency in any respect

4. the trader has charged for the goods mentioned in the complaint a price excess of the price fixed by or under any law for the time being in force or displayed on the goods or any package containing such goods.
5. goods which will be hazardous to life and safety when used, are being offered for sale to the public in contravention of the provisions of any law for the time being in force, requiring traders to display information in regard to the contents, manner and effect of use of such goods; with a view to obtaining any relief provided by law under the CPA.

Consumer means any person who:-

1. buys any goods for a consideration which has been paid or promised or partly paid and partly promised, or under any system of deferred payment (for example hire purchase or installment sales) and includes any other user of such goods when such use is made with the approval of the buyer, but does not include a person who obtains such goods for resale or for any commercial purpose; or
2. hires or avails of any services for a consideration which has been paid or promised, or partly paid and partly promised, or under any system of deferred payment and includes any beneficiary of such services when such services are availed of with the approval of the first mentioned person For the purposes of this definition "commercial purpose" does not include use by a consumer of goods bought and used by him exclusively for the purpose of earning his livelihood by means of self-employment.

Goods mean goods as defined in the Sale of Goods Act, 1930. Under that act, goods means every kind of movable property other than actionable claims and money and includes stocks and shares, growing crops, grass and things attached to or forming part of the land which are agreed to be severed before sale or under the contract of sale. Service is defined to mean service of any description which is made available to potential users and includes the provision of facilities in connection with banking, financing, insurance, transport, processing, supply of electrical or other energy, board or lodging or both, housing construction, entertainment, amusement or the purveying of news or other information but does not include the rendering of any service free of charge or under a contract of personal service. Consumer dispute means dispute where the person against whom a complaint has been made, denies or disputes the allegation contained in the complaint. Restrictive Trade Practice means any trade practice which requires a consumer to buy, hire, or avail of any good or as the case may be, services as a condition precedent for buying, hiring or availing of any other goods or services.

Unfair Trade Practice means unfair trade practice as defined under the Monopolies and Restrictive Trade Practices Act. The MRPT act has defined certain practices to be unfair trade practices.

Defect means any fault, imperfection or shortcoming in the quality, quantity, potency, purity or standard which is required to be maintained by or under any law for the time being in force or under any contract, express or implied, or as is claimed by the trade in any manner whatsoever in relation to any goods.

Deficiency means any fault, imperfection or shortcoming or inadequacy in the quality, nature and manner of performance which is required to be maintained by or under any law for the time being in force or has been undertaken to be performed by a person in pursuance of a contract or otherwise in relation to any service. A consumer is a user of goods and services. Any person paying for goods and services, which he uses, is entitled to expect that the goods and services be of a nature and quality promised to him by the seller.

The earlier principle of "Caveat Emptor" or "let the buyer beware" which was prevalent has given way to the principle of "Consumer is King". The origins of this principle lie in the fact that in today's mass production economy where there is little contact between the producer and consumer, often sellers make exaggerated claims and advertisements, which they do not intend to fulfill. This leaves the consumer in a difficult position with very few avenues for redressal. The onset on intense competition also made producers aware of the benefits of customer satisfaction and hence by and large, the principle of "consumer is king" is now accepted.

Objects of the Consumer Protection Act, 1986

The preamble to the Act states that the Act is legislated to provide for better protection of the interests of consumers and for that purpose to make provision for the establishment of consumer councils and other authorities for the settlement of consumer's disputes and for matters connected therewith. The CPA extends to the whole of India except the State of Jammu and Kashmir and applies to all goods and services unless otherwise notified by the Central Government. The basic rights of consumers as per the Consumer Protection Act (CPA) are:

1. Right to safety.
2. Right to be informed.
3. Right to choose.
4. Right to representation (or to be heard).
5. Right to seek redressal.
6. Right to consumer education.

1. *Right to Safety* It is the consumer right to be protected against goods and services which is hazardous to health or life.

2. *Right to be Informed* The consumer has the right to be informed about the quality, quantity, purity, standard and price of goods he intends to purchase. Therefore, the manufacture must mention complete information about the product, its ingredients, date of manufacture, price, precaution of use, etc. on the label and package of the product.

3. *Right to Choose* The consumer should be assured of freedom to choose from a variety of products at competitive prices. Every consumer wants to buy a product on his free will. There should be free competition in the market so that the consumer may make the right choice in satisfying his needs.

4. *Right to Representation (or to be Heard)* The consumer has a right to register dissatisfaction with any product and get his complaint heard.

   Most of the reputed firms have set up consumer service cells to listen to the consumer's complaint and take appropriate steps to redress their grievances.

5. *Right to Seek Redressal.* It is the right to seek redressal against any defect in goods or unfair trade suffered by the consumer. If the quality and performance of a product falls short of seller's claims, the consumer has a right to certain remedies.

   The Consumer Protection Act requires that the product must be repaired, replaced or taken back by the seller as provided under the contract between the buyer and the seller.

6. *Right to Consumer Education.* It means right of acquiring knowledge and being a well-informed consumer throughout his life. He should also be made aware of his rights and the remedies available through publicity in the mass media.

Consumer Responsibilities

(i) *To provide adequate information to the seller* The consumer has the responsibility to provide adequate information about his needs and expectation to the sellers.

(ii) *To exercise caution in purchasing* The consumer must try to get full information on the quality, design, utility, quantity, price, etc. of the product before purchasing it.

(iii) *To insist on cash memo or receipt* The consumer must get a cash memo or receipt as a proof of purchase of goods from the seller. This would help him in making a complaint to the seller in case of any defect in the goods.

(iv) *To file complaint against genuine grievance* The consumer must file a complaint with the seller or manufacturer about any defects or shortcoming in the products and services.

(v) *To be quality conscious* The consumer should never compromise on the quality of goods. While making purchases, the consumers must look for standard quality certification marks such as ISI, Agmark, Woolmark, FPO, etc. For example, electric iron must carry ISI mark.

Redressal Machinery under the Act

Consumer Protection Councils

The interests of consumers are enforced through various authorities set up under the CPA. The CPA provides for the setting up of the Central Consumer Protection Council, the State Consumer Protection Council and the District Forum.

Central Consumer Protection Council

The Central Government has set up the Central Consumer Protection Council, which consists of the following members:-

(a) The Minister in charge of Consumer Affairs in the Central Government who is its Chairman, and

(b) Other official and non-official members representing varied interests

The Central council consists of 150 members and its term is 3 years. The Council meets as and when necessary but at least one meeting is held in a year.

State Consumer Protection Council

The State Council consists of:-

(a) The Minister in charge of Consumer Affairs in the State Government who is its Chairman, and

(b) Other official and non-official members representing varied interests The State Council meets as and when necessary but not less than two meetings must be held every year.

Redressal Machinery under the Act

The CPA provides for a 3-tier approach in resolving consumer disputes.

The District Forum has jurisdiction to entertain complaints where the value of goods / services complained against and the compensation claimed is less than Rs. 20 lakhs, the State Commission for claims exceeding Rs. 20 lakhs but not exceeding Rs. 1crore and the National Commission for claims exceeding Rs.1 crore.

District Forum

Under the CPA, the State Government has to set up a district Forum in each district of the State. The government may establish more than one District Forum in a district if it deems fit. Each District Forum consists of:-

(a) A person who is, or who has been, or is qualified to be, a District Judge who shall be its President

(b) Two other members who shall be persons of ability, integrity and standing and have adequate knowledge or experience of or have shown capacity in dealing with problems relating to economics, law, commerce, accountancy, industry, public affairs or administration, one of whom shall be a woman.

Appointments to the State Commission shall be made by the State Government on the recommendation of a Selection Committee consisting of the President of the State Committee, the Secretary-Law Department of the State and the secretary in charge of Consumer Affairs Every member of the District Forum holds office for 5 years or up to the age of 65 years, whichever is earlier and is not eligible for re-appointment. A member may resign by giving notice in writing to the State Government whereupon the vacancy will be filled up by the State Government.

The District Forum can entertain complaints where the value of goods or services and the compensation, if any, claimed is less than rupees twenty lakhs. However, in addition to jurisdiction over consumer goods services valued upto Rs.20 lakhs, the District Forum also may pass orders against traders indulging in unfair trade practices, sale of defective goods or render deficient services provided the turnover of goods or value of services does not exceed rupees twenty lakhs. A complaint shall be instituted in the District Forum within the local limits of whose jurisdiction-

(a) The opposite party or the defendant actually and voluntarily resides or carries on business or has a branch office or personally works for gain at the time of institution of the complaint; or

(b) Any one of the opposite parties (where there are more than one) actually and voluntarily resides or carries on business or has a branch office or personally works for gain, at the time of institution of the complaint provided that the other opposite party/parties acquiescence in such institution or the permission of the Forum is obtained in respect of such opposite parties; or

(c) The cause of action arises, wholly or in part.

State Commission

The Act provides for the establishment of the State Consumer Disputes Redressal Commission by the State Government in the State by notification. Each State Commission shall consist of:-

(a) A person who is or has been a judge of a High Court appointed by State Government (in consultation with the Chief Justice of the High Court) who shall be its President;

(b) Two other members who shall be persons of ability, integrity, and standing and have adequate knowledge or experience of, or have shown capacity in dealing with, problems relating to economics, law, commerce, accountancy, industry, public affairs or administration, one of whom must be a woman.

Every appointment made under this is made by the State Government on the recommendation of a Selection Committee consisting of the President of the State Commission, Secretary-Law Department of the State and Secretary in charge of Consumer Affairs in the State.

Every member of the District Forum holds office for 5 years or upto the age of 65 years, whichever is earlier and is not eligible for re-appointment. A member may resign by giving notice in writing to the State Government whereupon the vacancy will be filled up by the State Government.

The State Commission can entertain complaints where the value of goods or services and the compensation, if any, exceeds Rs. 20 lakhs but does not exceed Rs. 1crore.

The State Commission also has the jurisdiction to entertain appeal against the orders of any District Forum within the State The State Commission also has the power to call for the records and appropriate orders in any consumer dispute which is pending before or has been decided by any District Forum within the State if it appears that such District Forum has exercised any power not vested in it by law or has failed to exercise a power rightfully vested in it by law or has acted illegally or with material irregularity.

National Commission

The Central Government provides for the establishment of the National Consumer Disputes Redressal Commission The National Commission shall consist of:-

(a) A person who is or has been a judge of the Supreme Court, to be appoint by the Central Government (in consultation with the Chief Justice of India) who be its President;

(b) Four other members who shall be persons of ability, integrity and standing and have adequate knowledge or experience of, or have shown capacity in dealing with, problems relating to economics, law, commerce, accountancy, industry, public affairs or administration, one of whom shall be a woman

Appointments shall be by the Central Government on the recommendation of a Selection Committee consisting of a Judge of the Supreme Court to be nominated by the Chief Justice of India, the Secretary in the Department of Legal Affairs and the Secretary in charge of Consumer Affairs in the Government of India.

Every member of the National Commission shall hold office for a term of five years or upto seventy years of age, whichever is earlier and shall not be eligible for reappointment. The National Commission shall have jurisdiction:-

a. to entertain complaints where the value of the goods or services and the compensation, if any, claimed exceeds rupees one crores:

b. to entertain appeals against the orders of any State Commission; and

c. to call for the records and pass appropriate orders in any consumer dispute which is pending before, or has been decided by any State Commission where it appears to the National Commission that such Commission has exercised a jurisdiction not vested in it by law, or has failed to exercise a jurisdiction so vested, or has acted in the exercise of its jurisdiction illegally or with material irregularity.

Complaints may be filed with the District Forum by:-

1. The consumer to whom such goods are sold or delivered or agreed to be sold or delivered or such service provided or agreed to be provided
2. Any recognized consumer association, whether the consumer to whom goods sold or delivered or agreed to be sold or delivered or service provided or agreed to be provided, is a member of such association or not
3. One or more consumers, where there are numerous consumers having the same interest with the permission of the District Forum, on behalf of or for the benefit of, all consumers so interested
4. The Central or the State Government.

On receipt of a complaint, a copy of the complaint is to be referred to the opposite party, directing him to give his version of the case within 30 days. This period may be extended by another 15 days. If the opposite party admits the allegations contained in the complaint, the complaint will be decided on the basis of materials on the record. Where the opposite party denies or disputes the allegations or omits or fails to take any action to represent his case within the time provided, the dispute will be settled in the following manner:-

In case of dispute relating to any goods: Where the complaint alleges a defect in the goods which cannot be determined without proper analysis or test of the goods, a sample of the goods shall be obtained from the complainant, sealed and authenticated in the manner prescribed for referring to the appropriate laboratory for the purpose of any analysis or test whichever may be necessary, so as to find out whether such goods suffer from any other defect.

The appropriate laboratory' would be required to report its finding to the referring authority, i.e. the District Forum or the State Commission within a period of forty-five days from the receipt of the reference or within such extended period as may be granted by these agencies.

Limitation Period for Filing of Complaint

The District Forum, the State Commission, or the National Commission shall not admit a complaint unless it is filed within two years from the date on which the cause of action has arisen. However, where the complainant satisfies the District Forum / State Commission, that he had sufficient cause for not filing the complaint within two years, such complaint may be entertained by it after recording the reasons for condoning the delay.

Powers of the Redressal Agencies

The District Forum, State Commission and the National Commission are vested with the powers of a civil court under the Code of Civil Procedure while trying a suit in respect of the following matters:-

1. The summoning and enforcing attendance of any defendant or witness examining the witness on oath;
2. The discovery and production of any document or other material producible as evidence;

3. The reception of evidence on affidavits:
4. The requisitioning of the report of the concerned analysis or test from the appropriate laboratory or from any other relevant source;
5. Issuing of any commission for the examination of any witness; and
6. Any other matter which may be prescribed.

Under the Consumer Protection Rules, 1987, the District Forum, Commission and the National Commission have the power to require any person:-

(i) To produce before, and allow to be examined by an officer of any authorities, such books of accounts, documents or commodities as may be required and to keep such book, documents etc. under its custody for the purposes of the Act;

(ii) To furnish such information which may be required for the purposes to any officer so specified.

They have the power to:-

(i) To pass written orders authorizing any officer to exercise power of entry and search of any premises where these books, papers, commodities, or documents are kept if there is any ground to believe that these may be destroyed, altered, falsified or secreted. Such authorized officer may also seize books, papers, documents or commodities if they are required for the purposes of the Act, provided the seizure is communicated to the District Forum / State Commission / National commission within 72 hours. On examination of such documents or commodities, the agency concerned may order the retention thereof or may return it to the party concerned.

(ii) to issue remedial orders to the opposite party.

(iii) to dismiss frivolous and vexatious complaints and to order the complainant to make payment of costs, not exceeding Rs. 10,000 to the opposite party.

Remedies Granted under the Act

The District Forum / State Commission / National Commission may pass one or more of the following orders to grant relief to the aggrieved consumer:-

1. To remove the defects pointed out by the appropriate laboratory from goods in question;
2. To replace the goods with new goods of similar description, which shall be free from any defect;
3. To return to the complainant the price, or, as the case may be, the charges paid by the complainant;
4. To pay such amount as may be awarded by it as compensation to the consumer for any loss or injury suffered by the consumer due to negligence of the opposite party;
5. To remove the defects or deficiencies in the services in question;
6. To discontinue the unfair trade practice or the restrictive trade practice or not to repeat them;
7. Not to offer the hazardous goods for sale:
8. To withdraw the hazardous goods from being offered for sale:
9. To provide for adequate costs to parties.

Appeals

Any person aggrieved by an order made by the Forum may prefer an appeal to the State Commission in the prescribed form and manner.

Similarly, any person aggrieved by any original order of the State Commission may prefer an appeal to the National

Commission in the prescribed form and manner. Any person aggrieved by any original order of the National Commission may prefer an appeal to the Supreme Court.

All such appeals are to be made within thirty days from the date of the order provided that the concerned Appellate authority may entertain an appeal after the said period of thirty days if it is satisfied that there was sufficient cause for not filling it within that period. The period of 30 days is to be computed from the date of receipt of the order by the appellant. Where no appeal has been preferred against any of the orders of the authorities, such orders would be final. The District Forum, State Commission or National Commission may enforce respective orders as if it was a decree or order made by a Court and in the event of their inability to execute the same; they may send the order to the Court for execution by it as if it were a Court decree or order.

Penalties

Failure or omission by a trader or other person against whom a complaint is made or the complainant to comply with any order of the State Commission or the National Commission shall be punishable with imprisonment for a term which shall not be less than one month but which may extend to 3 years, or with fine of not less than Rs. 2,000 but which may to Rs. 10000 or with both.

However, if it is satisfied that the circumstances of any case so requires, then the District Forum or the State Commission or the National Commission may impose a lower fine or a shorter term of imprisonment.

SUMMARY

During the mushrooming of insurance companies many financially unsound concerns were also floated which failed miserably.

The Insurance Act 1938 was the first legislation governing not only life insurance but also non-life insurance to provide strict state control over insurance business. The demand for nationalization of life insurance industry was made repeatedly in the past but it gathered momentum in 1944 when a bill to amend the Life Insurance Act 1938 was introduced in the Legislative Assembly.

However, it was much later on the 19th of January, 1956, that life insurance in India was nationalized. About 154 Indian insurance companies, 16 non-Indian companies and 75 provident were operating in India at the time of nationalization. Nationalization was accomplished in two stages; initially the management of the companies was taken over by means of an Ordinance, and later, the ownership too by means of a comprehensive bill. The Parliament of India passed the Life Insurance Corporation Act on the 19th of June 1956, and the Life Insurance Corporation of India was created on 1st September, 1956, with the objective of spreading life insurance much more widely and in particular to the rural areas with a view to reach all insurable persons in the country, providing them adequate financial cover at a reasonable cost.

The IRDA Bill provides for the establishment of an authority to protect the interests of the holders of insurance policies, to regulate, promote and insure orderly growth of the insurance industry and amend the Insurance Act, 1938, the Life Insurance Act, 1956 and the General Insurance Business (Nationalization) Act, 1972. The bill allows foreign equity stake in domestic private insurance companies to a maximum of 26 per cent of the total paid-up capital and seeks to provide statutory status to the insurance regulator. The insurance business in India is pegged at $ 6.6 Billion whereas industry leaders feel privatization will increase it to $ 40 Billion within next 3-5 years.

7

INSURANCE CONCEPTS IN GENERAL LIFE

INTRODUCTION

Insurance is system by which the losses suffered by a few are spread over many, exposed to similar risks. Insurance is a protection against financial loss arising on the happening of an unexpected event. Insurance policy helps in not only mitigating risks but also provides a financial cushion against adverse financial burdens suffered. Life is a roller coaster ride and is full of twists and turns. You cannot take anything for granted in life. Insurance policies are a safeguard against the uncertainties of life. Insurance policies cover the risk of life as well as other assets and valuables such as home, automobiles, jewelry et al. On the basis of the risk they cover, insurance policies can be classified into two categories:

Whole Life Insurance Policy, India

A whole life policy runs as long as the policyholder is alive. As risk is covered for the entire life of the policyholder, therefore, such policies are known as whole life policies. A simple whole life policy requires the insurer to pay regular premiums throughout the life. In a whole life policy, the insured amount and the bonus is payable only to the nominee of the beneficiary upon the death of the policyholder. There is no survival benefit as the policyholder is not entitled to any money during his / her own lifetime.

Term Life Insurance Policy, India

Term life insurance policy covers risk only during the selected term period.

If the policyholder survives the term, the risk cover comes to an end. Term life policies are primarily designed to meet the needs of those people who are initially unable to pay the larger premium required for a whole life or an endowment assurance policy.

No surrender, loan or paid-up values are granted under term life policies because reserves are not accumulated. If the premium is not paid within the grace period, the policy lapses without acquiring any paid-up value.

Money Back Policy, India

Money back policy provides for periodic payments of partial survival benefits during the term of the policy, as long as the policyholder is alive.

They differ from endowment policy in the sense that in endowment policy survival benefits are payable only at the end of the endowment period.

An important feature of money back policies is that in the event of death at any time within the policy term, the death claim comprises full sum assured without deducting any of the survival benefit amounts, which may have already been paid as money-back components. The bonus is also calculated on the full sum assured.

Joint Life Insurance Policy, India

Joint life insurance policies are similar to endowment policies as they too offer maturity benefits to the policyholders, apart form covering risks like all life insurance policies.

But joint life policies are categorized separately as they cover two lives simultaneously, thus offering a unique advantage in some cases, notably, for a married couple or for partners in a business firm.

Under a joint life policy the sum assured is payable on the first death and again on the death of the survivor during the term of the policy. Vested bonuses would also be paid besides the sum assured after the death of the survivor. If one or both the lives survive to the maturity date, the sum assured as well as the vested bonuses are payable on the maturity date. The premiums payable cease on the first death or on the expiry of the selected term, whichever is earlier.

Life Insurance, India

Life is very fragile and death is a certainty. We cannot control the uncertainties of life. But, we can cover the risks surrounding us. Life insurance, simply put, is the cover for the risks that we run during our lives. It protects us from the contingencies that could affect us.

Life insurance is not for the person who passes away, it for those who survive. It is the responsibility of every bread earner to guard against the events that could affect the family in the unfortunate circumstance of his / her demise. Thus, having a life insurance policy is very vital. Before going for a life insurance policy it is imperative that you know about various types of life insurance policies. Major among them are:

- Endowment Policy
- Whole Life Policy
- Term Life Policy
- Money-back Policy
- Joint Life Policy

- Group Insurance Policy
- Loan Cover Term Assurance Policy
- Pension Plan or Annuities
- Unit Linked Insurance Plan

Endowment Policy, India

An endowment policy covers risk for a specified period, at the end of which the sum assured is paid back to the policyholder, along with the bonus accumulated during the term of the policy. An endowment life insurance policy is designed primarily to provide a living benefit and only secondarily to provide life insurance protection. Therefore, it is more of an investment than a whole life policy.

Endowment life insurance pays the face value of the policy either at the insured's death or at a certain age or after a number of years of premium payment. Endowment policy is an instrument of accumulating capital for a specific purpose and protecting this savings program against the saver's premature death.

Group Insurance, India

Group insurance offers life insurance protection under group policies to various groups such as employers-employees, professionals, co-operatives, weaker sections of society, etc. It also provides insurance coverage for people in certain approved occupations at the lowest possible premium cost.

Group insurance plans have low premiums. Such plans are particularly beneficial to those for whom other regular policies are a costlier proposition. Group insurance plans extend cover to large segments of the population including those who cannot afford individual insurance.

A number of group insurance schemes have been designed for various groups. These include employer-employee groups, associations of professionals (such as doctors, lawyers, chartered accountants etc.), members of cooperative banks, welfare funds, credit societies and weaker sections of society.

Loan Cover Term Assurance Policy, India

Loan cover term assurance policy is an insurance policy, which covers a home loan. Such a policy covers the individual's home loan amount in case of an eventuality. The cover on such a policy keeps reducing with the passage of time as individuals keep paying their EMIs (equated monthly instalments) regularly, which reduces the loan amount.

This plan provides a lumpsum in case of death of the life assured during the term of the plan. The lumpsum will be a decreasing percentage of the initial sum assured as per the policy schedule. Since this is a non-participating (without profits) pure risk cover plan, no benefits are payable on survival to the end of the term of the policy.

Various insurance companies offering loan repayment protection insurance policy are

- HDFC Standard Life Insurance
- Tata AIG
- ING Vysya
- LIC

Pension Plan, India

A pension plan or an annuity is an investment that is made either in a single lump sum payment or through installments paid over a certain number of years, in return for a specific sum that is received every year, every half-year or every month, either for life or for a fixed number of years.

Annuities differ from all the other forms of life insurance in that an annuity does not provide any life insurance cover but, instead, offers a guaranteed income either for life or a certain period.

Typically annuities are bought to generate income during one's retired life, which is why they are also called pension plans. By buying an annuity or a pension plan the annuitant receives guaranteed income throughout his life. He also receives lump sum benefits for the annuitant's estate in addition to the payments during the annuitant's lifetime.

Unit Linked Insurance Plans (ULIP)

Unit linked insurance plan (ULIP) is life insurance solution that provides for the benefits of protection and flexibility in investment.

The investment is denoted as units and is represented by the value that it has attained called as Net Asset Value (NAV). The policy value at any time varies according to the value of the underlying assets at the time.

ULIP provides multiple benefits to the consumer. The benefits include:

- Life protection
- Investment and Savings
- Flexibility
- Adjustable Life Cover
- Investment Options
- Transparency
- Options to take additional cover against
- Death due to accident
- Disability
- Critical Illness
- Surgeries
- Liquidity
- Tax planning

General Insurance, India

General Insurance provides much-needed protection against unforeseen events such as accidents, illness, fire, burglary et al. Unlike Life Insurance, General Insurance is not meant to offer returns but is a protection against contingencies. Almost everything that has a financial value in life and has a probability of getting lost, stolen or damaged, can be covered through General Insurance policy.

Property (both movable and immovable), vehicle, cash, household goods, health, dishonesty and also one's liability towards others can be covered under general insurance policy. Under certain Acts of Parliament, some types of insurance like Motor Insurance and Public Liability Insurance have been made compulsory.

Major insurance policies that are covered under General Insurance are:

1-Home Insurance

2-Health Insurance

3-Motor Insurance

4-Travel Insurance

Home Insurance, India

Every man has a dream to own a house one day. For an ordinary person it takes a whole lifetime of savings to build a house. And one cannot predict a natural calamity like earthquake. In recent times we have seen what havoc an earthquake or any other natural calamity such as floods, landslides and torrential rains can wreck. Hence home insurance is very important. Home insurance policy also protects against other hazards like gas cylinder explosion, fire due to electric short circuit as well as man-made disaster like burglary.

Home insurance policy available in the market covers broadly two things:

- Building structure
- Contents inside the home

Insurance Covers for a Building Structure are:

The Fire and Special Perils Cover

This is a comprehensive packaged cover that covers damages to the structure of home due to

- Fire
- Storm, tempest, flood & inundation
- Riot, strike & malicious damage
- Lightning
- Explosion & implosion
- Aircraft damage
- Damage due to impact by vehicles
- Subsidence, landslides and rockslides
- Bursting and/or overflowing of water tanks, apparatus and pipes
- Missile testing operation
- Leakage from automatic Sprinkler installations
- Bush fire

Earthquake Cover

Covers damages to the structure of your house due to earthquake

Terrorism Cover

Covers damages to the structure of your house due to acts of terrorism. A home insurance does not cover the market value of the home. The price of the home includes the cost of the land and the cost of constructing the building structure on this land and the land cannot be insured. The insurance cover is only for the cost of constructing the building. The sum insured is calculated by multiplying your home area by the construction rate per sq. feet.

Insurance Cover for Contents Inside the Home

This cover is only for damages or loss of the contents inside the home-electronic and electrical goods, furniture and fixtures, clothing, jewelry and any other contents inside the home.

The covers that can be taken for the contents are as follows:

- The Fire and Specials Perils Cover
- Earthquake Cover
- Burglary
- Loss / damage to contents due to burglary or an attempted burglary
- Loss of jewelry, gold ornaments, silver articles and precious stones kept under lock & key

All the contents are covered on the market value of the items. This means that if there is a loss, the claim would be paid on the value of purchasing a similar new item, minus depreciation.

Health Insurance, India

It is said that a healthy mind resides in a healthy body. Hence it is very important to stay healthy. These days life is very fast and stressful. No matter how much you care one can always fall ill. Health treatment nowadays is very costly. More than the disease it is the cost of treatment that takes its toll. To get rid of health worries health / medical insurance is the answer. Health insurance policy not only covers expenses incurred during hospitalisation but also during the pre as well as post hospitalisation stages like money spent for conducting medical tests and buying medicines. The cover will be to the extent of the sum insured.

An added attraction of Mediclaim policies is the tax benefits which they attract under Section 80D. The maximum amount of deduction available under this section is Rs 10,000. In case of senior citizens, the maximum limit is Rs 15,000. Individuals also have the option of covering themselves for medical expenses by opting for the 'Critical Illness (CI)' rider available with life insurance policies.

Life insurance companies have their own list of critical illnesses as defined by them. In case of a CI rider, on the occurrence of a 'critical illness' during the policy tenure, an amount as proposed in the policy will be paid out to the individual. This is irrespective of the expenses incurred by the individual on hospitalisation, medicines and other such costs.

Health insurance companies are offering innovative products to their customers these days. The latest product in this line is 'cashless hospitalisation'. Here individuals do not have to pay for their hospital bills in case of hospitalisation; the insurance company settles the bill directly. But certain conditions like the hospital needs to have a tie-up with the insurance company, the documents need to be in order etc. have to be met.

Motor Insurance, India

Legally, no motor vehicle is allowed to be driven on the road without valid insurance. Hence, it is obligatory to get the vehicle insured.

Motor insurance policies cover against any loss or damage caused to the vehicle or its accessories due to the following natural and man made calamities.

Natural Calamities

Fire, explosion, self-ignition or lightning, earthquake, flood, typhoon, hurricane, storm, tempest, inundation, cyclone, hailstorm, frost, landslide, rockslide.

Man made Calamities

Burglary, theft, riot, strike, malicious act, accident by external means, terrorist activity, any damage in transit by road, rail, inland waterway, lift, elevator or air. Motor insurance provides compulsory personal accident cover for individual owners of the vehicle while driving. One can also opt for a personal accident cover for passengers and third party legal liability.

Third party legal liability protects against legal liability arising due to accidental damages. It includes any permanent injury / death of a person and damage caused to the property.

Travel Insurance, India

Travel and tourism is one of the most fast growing sectors around the world. With rise in standards of living, more and more people are embarking on journeys and exploring new places. Before going on a trip you need to address all your travel worries.

Travel insurance policy takes care of all your travel worries. It secures you and your loved ones in their sojourn abroad. Travel insurance plans offer host of benefits such as medical expenses, loss or delay of baggage or passport, personal accident, financial emergency assistance and hijack distress allowance. Travel insurance plans cover expenses incurred due to delayed flight, cancellation of trip, and also take care of valued assets left at home.

Insurance Companies in India

Before insurance sector was opened to the private sector Life Insurance Corporation (LIC) was the only insurance company in India. After the opening up of Insurance sector in India there has been a glut of insurance companies in India. These companies have come up with innovative and flexible insutrance policies to cater to varying needs of the individual. Opening up of the Insurance sector has also forced the Lic to tighten up its belt and deliver better service. All in all it has been a bonanza for the consumer.

Major Life insurance Companies in India are:

- Aviva Life Insurance
- Bajaj Allianz
- Birla S un Life Insurance
- HDFC Standard Life Insurance
- ICICI Prudential
- ING Vysya
- Kotak Mahindra
- LIC
- Max New York Life Insurance
- Metlife India Insurance
- Reliance Life Insurance
- SBI Life Insurance
- Shriram Life Insurance
- Tata AIG Life Insurance

HEALTH INSURANCE

Health insurance is a form of group insurance, where individuals pay premiums or taxes in order to help protect themselves from high or unexpected healthcare expenses.

Health insurance works by estimating the overall "risk" of healthcare expenses and developing a routine finance structure (such as a monthly premium, or annual tax) that will ensure that money is available to pay for the healthcare benefits specified in the insurance agreement.

The healthcare benefit is administered by a central organization, which is most often either a government agency, or a private or not-for-profit entity operating a health plan.

Market-based health care systems such as that in the United States rely heavily on private and not-for-profit health insurance.

HISTORY AND EVOLUTION

The concept of health insurance was proposed in 1694 by Hugh the Elder Chamberlen from the Peter Chamberlen family. In the late 19th century, "accident insurance" began to be available, which operated much like modern disability insurance.. This payment model continued until the start of the 20th century in some jurisdictions (like California), where all laws regulating health insurance actually referred to disability insurance. Patients were expected to pay all other health care costs out of their own pockets, under what is known as the fee-for-service business model.

During the middle to late 20th century, traditional disability insurance evolved into modern health insurance programs. Today, most comprehensive private health insurance programs cover the cost of routine, preventive, and emergency health care procedures, and also most prescription drugs, but this was not always the case.

OTHER FACTORS AFFECTING INSURANCE PRICES

A recent study by PriceWaterhouseCoopers examining the drivers of rising health care costs in the U.S. pointed to increased utilization created by increased consumer demand, new treatments, and more intensive diagnostic testing, as the most significant driver. People in developed countries are living longer.

The population of those countries is aging, and a larger group of senior citizens requires more intensive medical care than a young healthier population. Advances in medicine and medical technology can also increase the cost of medical treatment. Other factors that increase utilization and therefore insurance prices are lifestyle-related: increases in obesity caused by insufficient exercise and unhealthy food choices; excessive alcohol use, smoking, and use of street drugs. Other factors noted by the PWC study included the movement to broader-access plans, higher-priced technologies, and cost-shifting from Medicaid and the uninsured to private payers.

Common Complaints of Private Insurance

Some common complaints about private health insurance include:

1. Insurance companies usually only re-price their coverage annually. This means if one becomes ill, and is covered by a health insurance policy, and that illness will continue and be subject to a re-priced policy that person may find that their insurance premiums have increased to an amount they might not be able to afford. However, some states have rules and regulations which can limit price increases on certain types of health insurance coverage.
2. If insurance companies try to charge different people different amounts based on their own personal health, people may feel they are unfairly treated. Exceptions to this differential in pricing can be found when an individual (and their dependents) become insured under a pre-existing pool of insureds such as a group of employees insured through their employer. In that instance, the underwriter assesses the financial risk based upon the entire group (sometimes referred to as a 'risk pool').

   In these situations, a person with little or no medical expenses in their recent history will pay the same premium cost (and be subject to the same co-pays and deductibles) as someone who has had a large amount of medical expenses in their recent history.

3. When a claim is made, particularly for a sizable amount, insureds may feel as though the insurance company is using paperwork and bureaucracy to attempt to avoid payment of the claim or, at a minimum, greatly delay it. One large industry survey suggests that claim processing times improved between 2002 and 2006. More claims are being submitted electronically; however, 29 percent of claims were not received by the insurer until more than a month after the date on which medical care was provided. The percentage of claims being adjudicated on an automated basis is also increasing. 14 percent of claims are "pended" by the insurer while additional information is requested or the information on the claim is verified. On average, pended claims are delayed by 9 days. Over 95 percent of the remaining "clean" claims are processed within 30 days; 57 percent are processed within one week.
4. Health insurance is often only widely available at a reasonable cost through an employer-sponsored group plan and online for individuals.
5. In the United States, there are tax advantages to Employer-provided health insurance, whereas individuals must pay tax on income used to fund their own health insurance, although a small number of pre-tax health plans exist.
6. Experimental treatments are generally not covered. This practice is especially criticized by those who have already tried, and not benefited from, all "standard" medical treatments for their condition.
7. The Health Maintenance Organization (HMO) type of health insurance plan has been criticized for excessive cost-cutting policies in its attempt to offer lower premiums to consumers.

8. As the health care recipient is not directly involved in payment of health care services and products, they are less likely to scrutinize or negotiate the costs of the health care received. The health care company has popular and unpopular ways of controlling this market force.
9. Some health care providers end up with different sets of rates for the same procedure. One for people with insurance and another for those without.
10. Unlike most publicly funded health insurance, many private insurance plans do not provide coverage of dental health care, or only offer such coverage with additional premiums and very low dollar-amount coverages.
11. Insurance Companies can influence the type or amount of treatment that the insured receives by setting limits on the number of visits, types of treatment, etc., it will cover.

Health Insurance in the United States

According to the United States Census Bureau, approximately 84% of Americans have health insurance. Some 60% obtain health insurance through an employer, about 9% purchase it directly, and various government agencies provide coverage to about 27% of Americans (there is some overlap in these figures).

In 2006, there were 47 million people in the U.S. (16 percent of the population) who were without health insurance for at least part of that year. About 37% of the uninsured live in households with an income over $50,000.

Health insurers have a significant economic impact as employers-in 2004 they directly employed almost 470,000 people at an average salary of $61,409.

Medicare

In the United States, government-funded Medicare programs help to insure the elderly and end stage renal disease patients. Some health care economists (Uwe Reinhardt of Princeton and Stuart Butler among others) assert that (the third party payment feature) these programs have had the unintended consequence of distorting the price of medical procedures. As a result, the Health Care Financing Administration has set up a list of procedures and corresponding prices under the Resource-Based Relative Value Scale. Starting in 2006, Medicare Part D provides a program for the elderly to buy insurance for the purchase of prescription drugs.

Medicare Advantage

Medicare Advantage plans expand the health care options for Medicare beneficiaries. The option for Medicare Advantage plans is a result of the Balanced Budget Act of 1997, with the intent to better control the rapid growth in Medicare spending, as well as to provide Medicare beneficiaries more choices.

Medicaid

While Medicaid was instituted for the very poor, beginning in 1972, the number of individuals in the United States who lacked any form of health insurance for any period during the year increased each year, every year with the exceptions of the years 1999 and 2000. It has been reported that the number of physicians accepting Medicaid has decreased in recent years due to relatively high administrative costs and low reimbursements.

Private: Employer-sponsored

Health insurance paid for by business entities generally on behalf of their employees and other immediate stakeholders. Broadly classified as "Traditional/Indemnity" and "Managed/Preferred Provider." Most private health coverage in the U.S. is employment based, and the employer typically makes a substantial contribution towards the cost of coverage. Costs for employer-paid health insurance are rising rapidly: since 2001, premiums for family coverage have increased 78%, while wages have risen 19% and inflation has risen 17%, according to a 2007 study by the Kaiser Family Foundation.

According to the Centers for Medicare and Medicaid Services, nearly 100% of large firms offer health insurance to their employees. Although much more likely to offer retiree health benefits than small firms, the percentage of large firms offering these benefits fell from 66% in 1988 to 34% in 2002.

Common Health Insurance Terms

- *Annual Limit*-A benefit may be limited to a certain dollar or utilization limit (example: chiropractic care may be limited to 20 visits per calendar year).
- *Alternative Funding Arrangement*-A hybrid funding arrangement that features benefits of both self funding and fully insured arrangements (ASO, Minimum Premium, et. al.).
- *Birthday rule*-many insurance companies have adopted this rule to determine which parent is primary payer when both parents cover the same dependents. Who ever has the earlier date of birth, excluding the year, is designated primary insurance carrier. Exceptions to this rule usually arise when there is a court order for one of the parents to be the primary carrier.
- *Co-insurance*-Generally expressed as the percentage that you pay of any covered medical services after you have paid the deductible and co-pay.

- *Co-insurance limit*-The dollar amount you have to pay with Co-insurance before the insurance company begins paying your bills at 100% for the remainder of the plan year.
- *Co-ordination of benefits (COB)*-How your plan pays when it is coordinating with another plan. There are three principle methods in US health plans.
- *Co-pay*-A fixed fee you pay for services rendered. Most plans cover 100% after the co-pay for services rendered, however this can be adjusted to any amount depending on how the plan is set up.
- *Deductible*-The fixed amount you have to pay before your insurance starts to pay.
- *Deductible carry-forward*-Amounts for benefits incurred in the previous year may be subject to the prior year's deductibles.
- *Employee Assistance Plan*-a health-related benefit for non-medical, work-place issues or employees that commonly develop into medical issues such as marital counseling, absenteeism, suicidal ideation, etc.
- *Experimental/Investigational*-Most insurance companies will deny coverage for any procedures or tests which have not been medically verified by clinical trials conducted by recognized bodies of physicians or scientists. Many medical providers use tests which they believe in but have not been clinically validated.
- *Fully Insured*-The insurance company collects the premiums and pays claims from its own money.
- *Incurred But Not Paid (IBNP)*-under insurance based accrual accounting, a liability for claims that have not been paid, but may or may not be received. Incurred But Not Reported (IBNR) plus Reported But Not Paid (RBNP) equals IBNP. IBNP is a significant balance sheet item for insurers.

- *In-Network/Participating/Par Providers*-Medical providers who have an established relationship with an insurance company
- *Life time maximum*-The total your policy will pay out over the life of the contract. Many plans have a yearly restoration amount which will replenish the total so that after the policy money is exhausted there will still be some money in the following plan year for new claims. Life time maximums are easily avoided by switching policies or re-enrolling.
- *Self-Insured*-Many major U.S. and world corporations hire insurance companies and Third Party Administrators as claims and eligibility administrators to manage a health plan or trust. Many state laws do not apply to these plans due to ERISA exemption.
- *Reciprocity*-Most insurance plans deal with networks of doctors. If for example you have an HMO plan that allows you to see any HMO provider anywhere in the country, it is called Full Reciprocity, but if it only allows you access to local area networks of providers it is called Limited Reciprocity and if you can only go to select networks that your company has purchased access to, it is called No Reciprocity.
- *No-fault*-This is generally for automobile insurances, however if your auto policy is no-fault and you are injured, the medical insurance will become a secondary payer and will not be able to process claims until explanation of benefits are received from the auto insurance carrier.
- *Out-of-Network/Non Participating/Non-Par Providers*-Medical providers without an established relationship with an insurance company.
- *Out Of Pocket Maximum*-The total dollar amount paid out by a subscriber (deductible plus coinsurance).

- *Subscriber*-The primary member on the insurance policy. Also, "enrollee", "contractee".
- *Reserve*-refers to the amount that must be set aside for statutorily required funds for dissolution (terminal liability).

Health Insurance in Canada

Most health insurance in Canada is administered by each province, under the national law that requires all people to have free access to basic health services. Collectively, the public provincial health insurance systems in Canada are frequently referred to as Medicare. Private health insurance in Canada is allowed only for services that the public health plans do not cover; for example, semi-private or private rooms in hospitals and prescription drug plans. Canadians also must use private insurance for elective medical services such as Lasik surgery, plastic surgery such as liposuction, and other non-basic medical procedures. Private health insurance cannot cover physician fees which are covered by Medicare. Some 65% of Canadians have some form of supplementary private health insurance; many of them receive it through their employers. Private-sector services not paid for by the government account for nearly 30 percent of total health care spending. In 2005, the Supreme Court of Quebec ruled, in Chaoulli v. Quebec, that the prohibition on insurance for health care already insured by the state constitutes an infringement of the right to life and security. It is yet to be seen if this ruling will change the overall delivery of health insurance across Canada.

Health Insurance in Australia

The public health system is called Medicare. It ensures free universal access to hospital treatment and subsidised out-of-hospital medical treatment. It is funded by a 1.5% tax levy.

The private health system is funded by a number of private health insurance organisations. The largest of these is Medibank Private, which is government-owned, but operates as a government business enterprise under the same regulatory regime as all other registered private health funds. The Howard government has announced that Medibank will be privatised in 2008 assuming it is returned to office at the 2007 election; the Kevin Rudd-led Opposition has announced it will remain in government ownership if the Australian Labor Party wins.

Some private health insurers are 'for profit' enterprises, and some are non-profit organizations such as HCF Health Insurance. Some have membership restricted to particular groups, but the majority have open membership.

Most aspects of private health insurance in Australia are regulated by the Private Health Insurance Act 2007.

The private health system in Australia operates on a "community rating" basis, whereby premiums do not vary solely because of a person's previous medical history, current state of health, or (generally speaking) their age (but see Lifetime Health Cover below). Balancing this are waiting periods, in particular for pre-existing conditions (usually referred to within the industry as PEA, which stands for "pre-existing ailment"). Funds are entitled to impose a waiting period of up to 12 months on benefits for any medical condition the signs and symptoms of which existed during the six months ending on the day the person first took out insurance. They are also entitled to impose a 12-month waiting period for benefits for treatment relating to an obstetric condition, and a 2-month waiting period for all other benefits when a person first takes out private insurance. Funds have the discretion to reduce or remove such waiting periods in individual cases. They are also free not to impose them to begin with, but this would place such a fund at risk of "adverse selection", attracting a disproportionate number of members from other funds, or from the pool of intending members who might otherwise have joined other funds. It would also attract people with existing medical conditions, who might not otherwise have taken out insurance at all because of the denial of benefits for 12 months due to the PEA Rule. The benefits paid out for these conditions would create pressure on premiums for all the fund's members, causing some to drop their membership, which would lead to further rises, and a vicious cycle would ensue.

There are a number of other matters about which funds are not permitted to discriminate between members in terms of premiums, benefits or membership-these include racial origin, religion, sex, sexual orientation, nature of employment, and leisure activities. Premiums for a fund's product that is sold in more than one state can vary from state to state, but not within the same state.

The Australian government has introduced a number of incentives to encourage adults to take out private hospital insurance. These include:

- *Lifetime Health Cover*: If a person has not taken out private hospital cover by the 1st July after their 30th birthday, then when (and if) they do so after this time, their premiums must include a loading of 2% per annum. Thus, a person taking out private cover for the first time at age 40 will pay a 10 per cent loading. The loading continues for 10 years. The loading applies only to premiums for hospital cover, not to ancillary (extras) cover.
- *Medicare Levy Surcharge*: People whose taxable income is greater than a specified amount (currently $50,000 for singles and $100,000 for families) and who do not have an adequate level of private hospital cover must pay a 1% surcharge on top of the standard 1.5% Medicare Levy. The rationale is that if the people in this income group are forced to pay more money

one way or another, most would choose to purchase hospital insurance with it, with the possibility of a benefit in the event that they need private hospital treatment-rather than pay it in the form of extra tax as well as having to meet their own private hospital costs.

- *Private Health Insurance Rebate*: The government subsidises the premiums for all private health insurance cover, including hospital and ancillary (extras), by 30%, 35% or 40%.

Small Employer Group Coverage

According to a 2007 study, about 59% of employers at small firms (3-199 workers) in the U.S. provide employee health insurance, compared to 99% of large employers. The percentage of small firms offering coverage has been dropping steadily since 1999. The study notes that cost remains the main reason cited by small firms who do not offer health benefits.

The types of coverage available to small employers are similar to those offered by large firms, but small businesses do not have the same options for financing their benefit plans. In particular, self-insuring the benefits (see Self-funded health care) is not a practical option for most small employers.

States regulate small group premium rates, typically by placing limits on the premium variation allowable between groups (rate bands). Insurers price to recover their costs over their entire book of small group business while abiding by state rating rules.

Over time, the effect of initial underwriting "wears off" as the cost of a group regresses towards the mean-the average health status of the group eventually moves towards that of an average group. The process used to price small group coverage changes when a state enacts small group reform laws.

Insurance brokers play a significant role in helping small employers find health insurance, particularly in more competitive markets. Average small group commissions range from 2 percent to 8 percent of premiums. Brokers provide services beyond insurance sales, such as assisting with employee enrollment and helping to resolve benefits issues.

The Shift to Managed care in the U.S.

Through the 1990s, managed care grew from about 25% of U.S. employees with employer-sponsored coverage to the vast majority.

Private: Individually Purchased

Policies of health insurance obtained by individuals not otherwise covered under policies or programs elsewhere classified. Generally major medical, short term medical, and student policies. According to the U.S. Census Bureau, about 9% of Americans are covered under health insurance purchased directly. The range of products available is similar to those provided through employers. Average premiums are generally somewhat lower than those for employer-sponsored coverage, but vary by age. Deductibles and other cost-sharing are also higher, on average, and the individual consumer pays the entire premium without benefit of an employer contribution. Many states allow medical underwriting of applicants for individually purchased health insurance by insurance companies. A number of proposals have been advanced to limit the effect of underwriting on consumers and improve access to coverage. Each has its own advantages and limitations.

Private: long-term Care Insurance

Long-term care (LTC) insurance is growing in popularity in the U.S. Premiums have remained relatively stable in recent years. However, the coverage is quite expensive, especially when consumers wait until retirement age to purchase it. The average age of new purchasers was 61 in 2005, and has been dropping.

New Types of Medical Plans in the U.S.

One approach to addressing increasing premiums, dubbed "consumer driven health care," received a boost in 2003, when President George W. Bush signed into law the Medicare Prescription Drug, Improvement, and Modernization Act.

The law created tax-deductible Health Savings Accounts (HSAs). An HSA is a private bank account which is un-taxed and only penalized if spent on non-medical items or services. It must be paired with a high-deductible insurance plan. HSAs enable mostly healthy people to pay less for insurance and bank money for their own health care expenses. HSAs are one form of tax-preferenced health care spending account.

Others include Archer Medical Savings Accounts (MSAs), which have been superseded by the new HSAs (although existing MSAs are grandfathered), Flexible Spending Arrangements (FSAs) and Health Reimbursement Accounts (HRAs). FSAs and HRAs are typically used as part of an employee-benefit plan.

Limited Medical Benefit Plans pay for routine care and do not pay for catastrophic care. As such, they do not provide equivalent financial security to a major medical plan. Annual benefit limits can be as low as $2,000. Lifetime maximums can be very low as well.

HOW IT WORKS

A Health insurance policy is a contract between an insurance company and an individual. The contract can be renewable annually or monthly. The type and amount of health care costs that will be covered by the health plan are specified in advance, in the member contract or Evidence of Coverage booklet. The individual policy-holder's payment obligations may take several forms:

- *Premium*: The amount the policy-holder pays to the health plan each month to purchase health coverage.
- *Deductible*: The amount that the policy-holder must pay out-of-pocket before the health plan pays its share. For example, a policy-holder might have to pay a $500 deductible per year, before any of their health care is covered by the health plan.

  It may take several doctor's visits or prescription refills before the policy-holder reaches the deductible and the health plan starts to pay for care.
- *Copayment*: The amount that the policy-holder must pay out of pocket before the health plan pays for a particular visit or service. For example, a policy-holder might pay a $45 copayment for a doctor's visit, or to obtain a prescription. A copayment must be paid each time a particular service is obtained.
- *Coinsurance*: Instead of paying a fixed amount up front (a copayment), the policy-holder must pay a percentage of the total cost. For example, the member might have to pay 20% of the cost of a surgery, while the health plan pays the other 80%. Because there is no upper limit on coinsurance, the policy-holder can end up owing very little, or a significant amount, depending on the actual costs of the services they obtain.
- *Exclusions*: Not all services are covered. The policy-holder is generally expected to pay the full cost of non-covered services out of their own pocket.

- *Coverage limits*: Some health plans only pay for health care up to a certain dollar amount. The policy-holder may be expected to pay any charges in excess of the health plan's maximum payment for a specific service. In addition, some plans have annual or lifetime coverage maximums. In these cases, the health plan will stop payment when they reach the benefit maximum, and the policy-holder must pay all remaining costs.
- *Out-of-pocket maximums*: Similar to coverage limits, except that in this case, the member's payment obligation ends when they reach the out-of-pocket maximum, and the health plan pays all further covered costs. Out-of-pocket maximums can be limited to a specific benefit category (such as prescription drugs) or can apply to all coverage provided during a specific benefit year.

Prescription drug plans are a form of insurance offered through many employer benefit plans in the U.S., where the patient pays a copayment and the prescription drug insurance pays the rest.

Some health care providers will agree to bill the insurance company if patients are willing to sign an agreement that they will be responsible for the amount that the insurance company doesn't pay, as the insurance company pays according to "reasonable" or "customary" charges, which may be less than the provider's usual fee.

Health insurance companies also often have a network of providers who agree to accept the reasonable and customary fee and waive the remainder. It will generally cost the patient less to use an in-network provider.

Health Insurance companies are now offering Health Incentive accounts (HIA), to reward users for living healthy and making healthy choices, like stop smoking and/or losing weight, may get you funds added into your Health Incentive Account, which may lower your out of pocket costs. The health incentive accounts also carry over from year to year but once you leave the program you lose those benefits in the HIA.

Inherent Problems with Private Insurance

Any private insurance system will face two inherent challenges: adverse selection and ex-post moral hazard.

Adverse Selection

Insurance companies use the term "adverse selection" to describe the tendency for only those who will benefit from insurance to buy it. Specifically when talking about health insurance, unhealthy people are more likely to purchase health insurance because they anticipate large medical bills.

On the other side, people who consider themselves to be reasonably healthy may decide that medical insurance is an unnecessary expense; if they see the doctor once a year and it costs $250, that's much better than making monthly insurance payments of $400 (example figures).

The fundamental concept of insurance is that it balances costs across a large, random sample of individuals (see risk pool). For instance, an insurance company has a pool of 1000 randomly selected subscribers, each paying $100 per month.

One person becomes very ill while the others stay healthy, allowing the insurance company to use the money paid by the healthy people to pay for the treatment costs of the sick person.

However, when the pool is self-selecting rather than random, as is the case with individuals seeking to purchase health insurance directly, adverse selection is a greater concern. Adverse selection could leave an insurance company with primarily sick subscribers and no way to balance out the cost of their medical expenses with a large number of healthy subscribers.

Because of adverse selection, insurance companies employ medical underwriting, using a patient's medical history to screen out those whose pre-existing medical conditions pose too great a risk for the risk pool.

Before buying health insurance, a person typically fills out a comprehensive medical history form that asks whether the person smokes, how much the person weighs, whether the person has been treated for any of a long list of diseases and so on. In general, those who present a large financial burdens are denied coverage or charged high premiums to compensate.

One large U.S. industry survey found that roughly 13 percent of applicants for comprehensive, individually purchased health insurance who went through the medical underwriting in 2004 were denied coverage.

Declination rates increased significantly with age, rising from 5 percent for individuals 18 and under to just under a third for individuals aged 60 to 64.

Among those who were offered coverage, the study found that 76% received offers at standard premium rates, and 22% were offered higher rates. On the other side, applicants can get discounts if they do not smoke and are healthy.

Starting in 1976, some states started providing guaranteed-issuance risk pools, which enable individuals who are medically uninsurable through private health insurance to purchase a state-sponsored health insurance plan, usually at higher cost.

Minnesota was the first to offer such a plan; 34 states now offer them. Plans vary greatly from state to state, both in their costs and benefits to consumers and to their methods of funding and operations.

They serve a very small portion of the uninsurable market-about 182,000 people in the U.S. as of 2004, but in best cases allow people with pre-existing conditions such as cancer, diabetes, heart disease or other chronic illnesses to be able to switch jobs or seek self-employment without fear of being without health care benefits.

Efforts to pass a national pool have as yet been unsuccessful, but some federal tax money has been awarded to states to innovate and improve their plans.

Moral Hazard

Moral hazard occurs when two groups, an insurer and a consumer, enter into a contract under symmetric information, but one party takes action that is not taken into account in the contract, and changes the value of the insurance.

Co-payments, deductibles, and less generous insurance for services with more elastic demand combat moral hazard as they hold the consumer responsible. One example of moral hazard is the third party payment problem.

This occurs when the two parties involved in making a decision that affects how much something will cost are not responsible for bearing any of this cost.

One real life example would be a doctor and an insured patient agreeing to do unnecessary tests.

The doctor is happy because he possibly is paid more to run more tests, and failing that simply because he is preventing a possible malpractice suit by doing tests which might catch something he missed the first time around.

The patient is happy because she is now more sure than ever that nothing is wrong with her, and since it is at no cost to her, she doesn't mind the extra tests to be extra sure. The cost of these extraneous tests is borne by the insurance company, who had no say in the process what so ever.

BIBLIOGRAPHY

Campbell, J.Y., Lo, A.W.: *The Econometrics of Financial Markets,* Princeton University Press, 1996.

Chaudhuri, Pramit: *The Indian Economy: Poverty and Development,* New York, St. Martin's Press, 1979.

Dhingra, C.: *The Indian Economy: Resources, Planning, Development, and Problems,* Delhi, Sultan Chand, 1983.

Greer, Douglas F.: *Industrial Organization and Public Policy,* MacMillan Publishing Company, 1992.

Ishwar, C.: *The Indian Economy: Resources, Planning, Development, and Problems,* Delhi, Sultan Chand, 1983.

Little, I.M.D.: *India: Macroeconomics and Political Economy, 1964-1991,* Washington, World Bank, 1994.

Mongia, J.N.: *India's Economic Development Strategies, 1951-2000 A.D..* New Delhi, Allied, 1986.

Pranab, K.: *The Political Economy of Development in India,* Delhi, Oxford University Press, 1984.

Sargent, Thomas J.: *Dynamic Macroeconomic Theory,* Harvard University Press, 1987.

Tirole, Jean: *The Theory of Industrial Organization,* MIT Press, 1988.

Williamson, Jeffrey G.: *American Inequality: A Macroeconomic History,* New York, Academic Press, 1980.

Xavier Sala-i-Martin: *Economic Growth.* McGraw-Hill, 1995.

INDEX

A

Accident Benefit Policy, 233.
Agency Law, 196.
Alteration fee, 255.
Annuity policy, 233, 255.
Approach, 51, 80, 219.
Association, 101, 118, 156, 160, 165, 192, 195, 196, 210, 220.

B

Benefit Policy, 233.
Business Risks, 9, 13, 27.

C

Claim Settlement, 228, 239, 264, 265.
Commission, 90, 91, 144, 159, 163, 166, 167, 168, 178, 179, 195, 205, 210, 216, 217, 218, 219, 220, 221, 222, 223, 224, 225.
Committee, 88, 118, 119, 120, 121, 122, 135, 137, 138, 141, 157, 186, 191, 192, 217, 218, 219.
Community, 85, 95, 99, 154, 160, 229.
Company, 5, 20, 35, 36, 37, 65, 67, 69, 70, 71, 72, 74, 75, 76, 82, 83, 89, 90, 91, 92, 93, 94, 100, 103, 113, 114, 117, 118, 119, 120, 121, 123, 124, 125, 126, 127, 128, 129, 130, 135, 137, 140, 142, 143, 160, 161, 163, 164, 165, 166, 167, 169, 175, 176, 177, 183, 193, 195, 227, 228, 229, 231, 236, 237, 238, 239, 240, 242, 245, 246.
Consumer, 3, 4, 9, 10, 12, 16, 26, 32, 34, 61, 67, 73, 74, 80, 129, 138, 192, 210, 211, 212, 213, 214, 215, 216, 217, 218, 219, 220, 222, 223.
Consumer Protection Act, 210, 213, 214.
Consumer Risks, 10, 16.
Corporation, 31, 67, 88, 90, 91, 93, 94, 95, 117, 118, 122, 124, 125, 127, 128, 131, 132, 134, 135, 136, 137, 139, 140, 141, 142, 143, 144, 146, 150, 152, 153, 154, 155,

156, 157, 158, 159, 160, 161, 162, 163, 164, 180, 225, 230.
Culture, 141.

D

Death Claims, 227, 229.
Department, 135, 137, 141, 217, 218, 220, 244, 247, 248.
Development, 1, 88, 90, 100, 123, 128, 132, 133, 134, 136, 138, 146, 161, 162, 164, 166, 168, 169, 180, 187, 190, 192, 193, 194, 230.
Distribution, 23, 130, 132, 265.
Documentation, 228, 235.
Double Accident Benefit Policy, 233.

E

Employment, 14, 30, 73, 78, 86, 101, 177, 183, 211, 263, 266, 267.
Endorsements, 238, 257.
Endowment Life Policy, 232.
Environment, 28, 29, 38, 123, 131, 132, 138, 142, 266.
Evolution, 68, 266.

F

Financial Markets, 5, 38, 39, 43.
Financial Planning, 1.

G

Government, 2, 15, 18, 21, 22, 30, 31, 33, 37, 38, 40, 41, 43, 50, 68, 77, 84, 85, 86, 87, 88, 91, 92, 117, 118, 119, 120, 121, 122, 123, 125, 127, 131, 134, 138, 139, 150, 152, 153, 154, 157, 158, 159, 160, 161, 162, 163, 164, 168, 169, 170, 171, 172, 173, 174, 180, 181, 182, 183, 186, 187, 188, 189, 190, 191, 210, 213, 216, 217, 218, 219, 220, 221, 262, 267.
Group Insurance, 57, 59, 68, 108, 132, 133, 235.

H

Health Insurance, 3, 10, 11, 14, 15, 21, 22, 23, 24, 25, 31, 32, 34, 36, 37, 40, 42, 62, 64, 65, 68, 69, 71, 72, 73, 74, 75, 76, 77, 78, 79, 80, 81, 84, 85, 87, 108, 113, 124, 232, 265.

I

Industry, 2, 3, 9, 21, 27, 37, 39, 40, 46, 72, 75, 85, 89, 92, 93, 95, 96, 101, 110, 111, 117, 119, 120, 121, 123, 131, 142, 145, 180, 190, 192, 217, 218, 219, 225, 226, 245, 265, 266, 267.
Insurance, 1, 2, 3, 4, 5, 6, 7, 8, 9, 10, 11, 12,

13, 14, 15, 16, 17, 18, 19, 20, 21, 22, 23, 24, 25, 26, 27, 28, 29, 30, 31, 32, 33, 34, 35, 36, 37, 38, 39, 40, 41, 42, 43, 46, 56, 57, 58, 59, 60, 61, 62, 63, 64, 65, 66, 67, 68, 69, 70, 71, 72, 73, 74, 75, 76, 77, 78, 79, 80, 81, 82, 83, 84, 85, 86, 87, 88, 89, 90, 91, 92, 93, 94, 95, 96, 97, 98, 99, 100, 101, 102, 103, 104, 105, 106, 107, 108, 109, 110, 111, 112, 113, 114, 115, 116, 117, 118, 119, 120, 121, 122, 123, 124, 125, 126, 127, 128, 129, 130, 131, 132, 133, 134, 135, 136, 139, 142, 143, 144, 145, 146, 147, 148, 149, 150, 151, 152, 154, 155, 158, 159, 160, 161, 162, 163, 164, 165, 166, 167, 168, 169, 170, 171, 172, 173, 174, 175, 177, 178, 179, 180, 181, 182, 183, 184, 185, 186, 187, 189, 190, 191, 192, 193, 194, 212, 225, 226, 227, 228, 229, 230, 231, 232, 235, 236, 237, 238, 239, 240, 241, 244, 245, 246, 247, 251, 253, 256, 257, 258, 259, 260.

J

Joint Life Policy, 57, 59, 233.

L

Life Insurance Contract, 98, 227, 228, 229.

Life Insurance Corporation, 67, 88, 90, 91, 93, 94, 95, 117, 118, 122, 125, 128, 146, 150, 152, 164, 180, 225, 230.

Life Insurers, 16, 88, 89, 93, 125, 127.

Life Policy, 57, 58, 59, 230, 231, 232, 233.

M

Majority, 4, 35, 42, 79, 85, 147, 184, 196, 250.

Maturity Claims, 227, 242, 243.

Money Back Policy, 58, 235.

N

Nomination, 185, 239, 242, 247, 249, 250, 251.

O

Opportunity, 95, 123, 141, 156, 184, 190, 195.

Organization, 68, 76, 94, 95, 113.

P

Pension Plan, 57, 60, 61, 109, 139.

Policy, 2, 15, 17, 18, 21, 23, 27, 28, 29, 39, 41, 51, 56, 57, 58, 59, 60, 61, 62, 63, 65, 66, 69, 70, 74, 83, 84, 89, 93,

94, 95, 97, 98, 99, 101, 102, 103, 105, 106, 108, 109, 110, 113, 114, 115, 116, 118, 119, 120, 124, 126, 131, 135, 137, 138, 139, 143, 145, 146, 148, 149, 162, 179, 185, 188, 228, 230, 231, 232, 233, 234, 235, 236, 237, 238, 239, 240, 241, 242, 243, 244, 245, 246, 247, 248, 249, 250, 251, 252, 253, 254, 255, 256, 257, 258, 259.

Premium Payment, 57, 97.

Premium Receipt, 237, 247.

Production, 175, 188, 213, 222.

Profit Policy, 233.

Property, 4, 12, 13, 14, 26, 27, 32, 62, 66, 99, 103, 104, 105, 106, 108, 109, 110, 111, 112, 113, 115, 124, 153, 155, 167, 173, 181, 195, 200, 205, 212, 255.

Proposal Forms, 236, 245.

Protection, 15, 17, 29, 56, 57, 59, 60, 61, 62, 107, 109, 112, 154, 160, 165, 185, 190, 202, 210, 213, 214, 215, 216, 222, 228, 230, 232.

Provisions, 9, 28, 90, 97, 145, 150, 153, 154, 159, 160, 161, 170, 171, 175, 176, 177, 179, 181, 182, 185, 188, 189, 190, 193, 194, 196, 200, 210, 211.

R

Research, 16, 17, 21, 23, 192, 266.

Resolution, 93, 180.

Risk Manager, 1, 2.

S

Society, 1, 59, 60, 92, 100, 109, 110, 117, 123, 134, 152, 163, 165, 166, 230, 258, 259.

T

Technology, 26, 54, 74, 95, 121, 130, 136.

Term Policy, 231.

W

Welfare, 60, 116, 134, 141.

Whole Life Policy, 57, 58, 231, 232.

□□□